C000261939

# BOGOTÁ BANDIT

Richard Adamson is a freelance journalist and ghost writer who lectures in media studies at Westminster University and for the National Council for Training of Journalists at Lambeth College, London. He also acts an editorial consultant to the New Sabah Times Group in Malaysia and the *Camden New Journal* in north London. During a varied career as a print and TV journalist, he has worked for, among others, *London Tonight*, Granada, LWT and Central TV, the *Daily Telegraph*, *The Guardian*, the *Sunday Times*, *The Independent*, the *Daily* and *Sunday Express*, the *Daily Mail*, the *Daily Star*, the *Sunday People*, the *Sunday Mirror Magazine*, IPC magazines, the *Manchester Evening News* and the North Wales *Evening Leader*.

He was a Hertfordshire County schoolboy cap and went on to play as an amateur in North Wales junior soccer for Holywell Town, Mostyn and Buckley Wanderers. He was watched by several League-club scouts, but they subsequently kept their distance – he likes to think because his manager was asking for too big a bung . . .

# BOGOTÁ BANDIT

### The Outlaw Life of Charlie Mitten:
### Manchester United's Penalty King

**RICHARD ADAMSON**

MAINSTREAM
PUBLISHING
EDINBURGH AND LONDON

For Dan and Dom

This edition, 2005

Copyright © Richard Adamson, 1996
All rights reserved
The moral right of the author has been asserted

First published in Great Britain in 1996 by
MAINSTREAM PUBLISHING COMPANY
(EDINBURGH) LTD
7 Albany Street
Edinburgh EH1 3UG

ISBN 1 84596 065 3

No part of this book may be reproduced or transmitted in
any form or by any means without written permission
from the publisher, except by a reviewer who wishes to
quote brief passages in connection with a review written
for insertion in a magazine, newspaper or broadcast

A catalogue record for this book is available
from the British Library

Typeset in Gill Sans and Janson
Printed and bound in Great Britain by
Cox & Wyman Ltd

# Contents

Old men forget; yet all shall be forgot,
But he'll remember with advantages
What feats he did that day.
*Henry V*, Act IV, Scene III

# Foreword

CHARLIE MITTEN WAS A UNIQUE FOOTBALL CHARACTER, A man not only of his times but the ages, and his story, so colourfully told by Richard Adamson, would be fascinating in any epoch.

However, against the backcloth of today's rampant football wealth – when Rio Ferdinand coolly renegotiates a £100,000-a-week contract in the wake of an eight-month, fully paid suspension for failing to take a drugs test and the splendid Frank Lampard casually reveals that thieves stole £172,000 that happened to be lying around his house in one of the prime corners of west London – Mitten's fight for decent rewards at a time when the great stadiums of English football groaned with crowds of 60–70,000 almost defies credibility.

Mitten was a rebel and a star. He was also arguably Manchester United's best pure winger – if we carefully detach George Best from that strict category – and also one of those men who, tempered by war, gave the football of the late 1940s and early '50s such fine character.

Even Sir Matt Busby, so unforgiving of Mitten's decision to defect from United for the superior wages offered by the Colombian club Santa Fé, had a soft spot for 'Cheeky' Charlie. The great Alfredo di Stefano, a teammate of Mitten's in Bogotá before Colombia joined the FIFA fold, told Adamson of his great admiration for the man who saw himself, so legitimately, as a great entertainer deserving better wages than some worthy tradesmen.

Inevitably, that insistent belief of Mitten's that he was being grievously short-changed provides the core of the story Adamson has to tell, but then he also takes full advantage of the fact that Mitten was much more than a talented footballer with a cause. He was full of life and humour and conviction and never more so than when he stepped up to take a penalty. From the spot, as much as when he was under pressure on the flank, he was deadly.

His story is recommended to anyone who cares about football and not least some of today's superstars who so often perform in a way that would have shamed Mitten and his teammates.

*James Lawton*
*Chief Sports Writer at* The Independent

# Preface to the 1996 Edition

LIKE MANY GOOD STORIES, THIS ONE BEGAN IN THE VILLAGE barber's shop. It was a chance remark by Ron Keeling at his salon in Chorlton-cum-Hardy, Manchester, barely a mile from Old Trafford, that sparked the quest which led to this book. How is it that so many practitioners of this illustrious profession seem to have a folk memory stretching back to the Middle Ages, and a client list that reads like a local *Who's Who*? Well, there I was, at the height of the 1994–95 season, having my regular trim and exchanging idle chatter about England's finest, Manchester United and Blackburn Rovers – who were then being taught a lesson in the European Champions League – when Ron let slip, in the conspiratorial way barbers do, that United's Bogotá Bandit would have something to say about the English clubs' dismal showing. 'Charlie who?' I can still hear myself asking incredulously. Now I know how Accrington Stanley supporters feel. So it was that I embarked on a real-life El Dorado quest. En route, I was to discover the story of a soccer outlaw and visionary, one of the most electrifying players England never had. It's a tale with a script which even Hollywood wouldn't have dared dream up. Curious? So was I . . .

No story like this can be written without the absolutely invaluable help of those who've trodden this way before, and I readily express my gratitude to, in particular, the *Sunday Times Chronicle of Twentieth-Century Sport* (WH Smith) by Chris Nawrat, Steve Hutchings and Greg Struthers, the *Daily Telegraph Football Chronicle* (Stanley Paul) by Norman Barrett, the *Sunday Times Illustrated History of Football* (Hamlyn) by Chris Nawrat and Steve Hutchings, the *Guinness Book of World Soccer* (Guinness Publishing), *For the Good of the Game: the Official History of the PFA* (Robson Books) by John Harding, *Soccer at Home and Abroad* (Stanley Paul) by Neil Franklin, *Don't Shoot the Manager* (Boxtree) by Jimmy Greaves and Norman Giller, *The Gibson Guarantee: the Saving of Manchester United* (Imago Publishing) by Peter Harrington, *Sir Matt Busby: the Official Authorised Biography* (Virgin) by Rick Glanvill and *A Kick in the Right Direction: Coaching and the Professional Game, the Final Report of the PFA Working Party*. I would also like to express my thanks for the help so graciously given by so many individuals to assist my quest, whether to offer comments and insights, answer queries, or help chase up the obscure facts which are the building blocks of any good yarn: staff of the embassy of the Republic of Colombia, London; Jack Rollin, soccer reference book supreme; Paul Power of the PFA's coaching secretariat in Manchester; David Barber and Andrin Cooper of the FA press office; Catherine Smith of the Scottish FA media office; Cliff Butler, as editor of the *Manchester United Review*; and Mike Cox, Johnny Anderson, Henry Cockburn, Allenby Chilton, Johnny Morris and Stan Pearson; Johnny Haynes, Bedford Jezzard and Beryl Franklin; Melvyn Tanner, chairman Fulham 2000; David Sadler; Jack Retter, Mansfield Town contributor to the PFA

Factfile and author of the *Centenary History of Mansfield Town FC*; John Lomas, sports editor of the *Mansfield Chronicle and Advertiser*; John Gibson, executive sports editor of the *Newcastle Evening Chronicle*; Joe 'Mr Mansfield' Eaton; Aston Villa archivist David Goodyer; Neil Benson, editor-in-chief of the *Newcastle Journal* and *Evening Chronicle*; Andrea Whittaker, Alfredo di Stefano and Angela Marti; Sir Stanley Matthews, Bobby Robson, Ian St John and Patrick Barclay of the *Sunday Telegraph*; Jim Hooley, chief sports sub-editor of the *Daily Mail*; Martina Anzinger; my brother Patrick; Paul Cahill of the North East Macintosh User Group for his technical assistance; and last but not least to the late, great 'Cheeky' Charlie Mitten for his unfailing courtesy and patience.

For a blow-by-blow account of all those things you always suspected were wrong with the English game and which have been so tantalisingly left out of this tale, I recommend Alex Fynn and Lynton Guest's bestselling, brilliantly stitched-together cornucopia of insights, *Out of Tune: Why Football Isn't Working* (Pocket Books).

Finally, if any errors have got through my *catenaccio* double-checking, they are, of course, all my own work.

# INTRODUCTION TO THE SECOND EDITION

# Chronicles of Sudden Death Foretold

> Any half-decent penalty-taker should be able to beat the goalkeeper blindfolded.
>
> Charlie Mitten, 1995

Once met, never forgotten: that was the man I had the privilege to get to know quite by chance in 1994 and '95. The result was the first edition of this book in 1996. Charlie rejoiced in its publication: when he invited me to tell his story, he told me that to write the biography of his life had been a secret ambition for almost 30 years. But the first edition didn't include the blindfold claim by the man known throughout the beautiful game for almost half a century as 'Cheeky' Charlie Mitten. It seemed like an acerbic opinion too far. How wrong can you be?

And, yes, I too would have died wondering, had I not had the chance to test Mitten's most outrageous theory. Here are his exact words:

'It should be a certainty, this kick; it's the easiest of the match. Yet come the penalties, they [the players] say they can't do it – it's the big occasion. But if you can do it automatically, you don't need to think about it – you can do it blindfolded.

'Penalties are crucial – [they] can decide a game. Premiership players – professional footballers earning £25,000 a week – should be able to step up to the ball and knock it straight into the corner [of the net]. They should be able to take the lace out at the same time.'

Irreverent to the last, Charlie Mitten never lost his talent for providing an interesting quote. Weeks after the book was published, I was able to put his astonishing blindfold claim to the test. It turned out to be true, confirming what so many people who knew Manchester United's all time greatest outside-left had told me: that never in Cheeky Charlie Mitten's illustrious career did he ever spin anyone a line.

So it was that I accompanied Mitten to Maine Road – at one time Manchester United's home ground – the scene of many of Charlie's glory games. Our volunteers were two of City's promising teenagers who had both made first-team appearances. They each scored blindfolded from the spot after just five minutes' one-to-one instruction by Charlie. Incredible? To be sure. I wouldn't have believed it either, if I hadn't seen it with my own eyes.

Charlie and this writer kept in touch as the century drew to a close and the new one began, and in our chats, his sharp, perspicacious comments were never less than enlightening and entertaining – especially with regards to the 1998 World Cup and Euro 2000. I know he was looking forward to the 2002 World Cup in Korea and Japan, and it was with great sadness that I learned of his death in January 2002, two weeks short of his eighty-second birthday.

Charlie's penalty-taking record, which lasted more than 50 years, has now gone as well. As Sir Alex told me in 1995, when Eric Cantona and Steve Bruce met up with Charlie at United's training ground for this book: 'Charlie's is a hell of a record – it will be hard to beat.' But it was beaten and a new penalty king has been anointed by Alex Ferguson. And Charlie Mitten would have been the first to hail Ruud van Nistelrooy's feat.

For Cheeky Charlie, converting spot-kicks had nothing to do with 'Lady Luck' – as he proved in five glorious seasons as Manchester United's dead-ball specialist and first penalty king. Only Steve Bruce – now manager of Birmingham City – and Eric Cantona came close before van Nistelrooy, but both left Old Trafford before they could assume Charlie's spot-kick accolade. Bruce notched up 17 successful spot-kicks by the time he transferred to Birmingham City and Cantona 15 before the movies beckoned Old Trafford's philosopher king. Denis Irwin took on the role and was going well with 12 scores, when his time in the top flight ran out, and he was transferred to Wolves in 2002. Then came Beckham, Scholes, et al., who all had a go, before the job was handed to the flying Dutchman.

But even Charlie's successor as the most successful penalty marksman at the 'Theatre of Dreams' finds scoring from the spot a hit-and-miss affair, it seems. At the start of the 2005–06 season, Ruud van Nistelrooy was on 20 but firing as many blanks as hits. His boss puts van Nistelrooy's inconsistency down to pressure. After his hit-man had his spot-kick saved by Bolton's Jussi Jaaskelainen in the season's opening game, Sir Alex remarked that possibly 'missing two prior to this one played on his mind and that's why he hit it so hard'.

Van Nistelrooy is not alone. In the Carling Cup in October 2005, Robert Huth dented Chelsea's new-found aura of invincibility by failing in the shoot-out that saw Charlton through, while in September, Manchester City were blown out of the Carling Cup 3–0 by Doncaster Rovers in the sudden-death shoot-out after a 1–1 extra-time draw. And there are sure to be many more examples before the season is out – both in the Premiership and Champions League.

The failure of so many players – especially in sudden-death shoot-outs at the highest level in the European Cup and the World Cup finals – demonstrates what a nerve-racking business the spot-kick is. A missed penalty can have devastating consequences on soccer's glory trail – sudden death for your reputation, for your club and even for your country.

The examples are legendary – most soccer supporters could quote a horror story visited on their club by the *Elfmeterschiessen*, and many an England fan will be looking with foreboding to the World Cup, which in 2006 will be played out on the Bundesliga grounds of Germany. Any bets on the shooters who will condemn their country to sudden-death elimination in the heart-stopping spectacle that is the penalty shoot-out?

It's worth emphasising that word 'spectacle', because, arguably, the shoot-out is the greatest innovation in the game since, well, the invention of the penalty itself. The original penalty-kick was introduced in the 1890–91 season to punish a team for a foul so heinous that it merited a free goal to the wronged side. The 12-yard free-kick was considered a mere formality, but, initially, many teams refused to even try to score from a penalty because they considered such a goal unworthy of gentlemanly conduct. Even the illustrious Pelé is on the record as saying that the penalty is a 'cowardly' way to score. Although that didn't stop him from practising assiduously; he was never a 'welly it anywhere' merchant. For Pelé, like Charlie Mitten, believed that even the simplest kick in the game needs practice to hone pitch-perfect technique.

Penalties at the end of a drawn game were introduced because an increasing number of all-square ties were being decided on the drawing of lots or the toss of a coin, especially as knockout cup soccer went European from 1955 onwards. What's that about the sudden-death shoot-out being 'unfair' or 'unsatisfactory', as so many pundits aver?

So the shoot-out was born in 1970 – in the old Watneys Cup in a tie between Hull City and . . . guess who? Man United! And who was the first player to score in a shoot-out? Step forward George Best. And the first to miss? Denis Law, with penalty number four. You couldn't make this stuff up.

Football ain't rocket science, brain surgery or running the country – it's theatre. The exciting moments in most matches don't add up to a hill of beans: you are lucky to get five, six, seven or maybe even eight minutes of thrilling action in total. Check it out on your next visit to your own 'theatre of dreams'. And if football isn't theatrical, what's the point of watching? Yeah, yeah, but after tribal loyalty, what?

The fact is, the penalty shoot-out has injected a new level of nerve-tingling frisson into the game which has captured the imagination of even soccer phobics. More than 26 million people in Britain watched the shoot-out against Germany in Euro '96 – one of the largest TV-viewing figures on record. And they were rewarded with a piece of monstrously compelling theatre – the redemption and absolution of Stuart Pearce. Shower curtains? Give me the antics of the 'Soccer Psycho' any day.

Charlie Mitten always insisted that the shoot-out separated the true masters from the journeymen at the highest level. And to suggest penalty-taking is a 'lottery', as many pundits do, is as wide of the mark as so many spot-kicks. Perhaps even Thierry Henry betrayed something of this way of thinking when he summed up the Pires penalty farce at Highbury in 2005: 'You do have to wonder what can happen to your mind with penalties.'

When asked after the 2005 FA Cup final shoot-out against Manchester United if his players had practised, Arsène Wenger replied: 'Yes, yes, a little bit . . . but you can't really prepare for something like this.' Charlie would have had some blunt advice for the Gunners manager. He probably would have referred him to Spurs' Jermaine Jenas, who scored a 30-yard free-kick screamer to ensure the spoils were shared in the early 2005–06 season north-London derby with Arsenal: 'Taking free-kicks is all about what you do in training.'

Even hit-man Alan Shearer's verdict that 'it really does take courage to get up and take one' wouldn't have done for Charlie. He always dismissed the idea that any special talent was needed or that iron-willed control of nerves was the main thing. The true secret, he insisted, lay elsewhere, as we shall see.

This book began as a magazine article in 1994 and took on a life of its own. In writing Charlie Mitten's biography, I discovered a true soccer legend – and, to my surprise (and initial disbelief), I came to agree with his conclusion that even successful penalties these days are largely speculative lunges: hit or miss affairs, even by the best players. Mitten's explanation was that most penalty-kicks are lacking in purposeful technique. If true, this is surely soccer's biggest open secret: that most players, even among the best in the world, don't know the best way to take a penalty-kick – no ifs; no buts.

Whether he was right, I'll leave you, the reader, to decide, as I invite you on a journey to discover the story of a man who, in a colourful life, truly graced the beautiful game.

# I

# Charlie Who?

Football is not really about winning, or goals, or supporters
– it's about glory.

Danny Blanchflower, League and FA Cup
Double-winning Spurs skipper, 1961

THOSE WHO COME TODAY TO DO BATTLE ON THE LUSH
playing field of Medellín best tread softly and carry something
more than a big stick. For even an away-fixture trip to this
sprawling Andean town in the heart of cocaine country could
prove a hazardous affair. The murder of Andreas Escobar –
shot dead for the own-goal which put out favourites Colombia
in the 1994 World Cup – shows that soccer, like much else,
has become something more than a matter of life and death.

But for one Englishman at least, Colombia's modern-day
notoriety and venal passion for violence never obscured fond
memories of a beautiful country, where he helped write a
footnote to the history of the beautiful game. Money seemed
to grow on trees: ripening coffee beans and bananas festooned
every avenue, every dusty road; orange and grapefruit groves
and banana plantations stretched all the way up the
mountainsides as far as the eye could see. Groves and

plantations were laced by cool streams, and beautiful tropical vegetation was studded everywhere with wild orchids. And in the thronging, chanting football crowds were the most beautiful women in the world.

That was how it looked to one English exile 55 years ago, when all-seater stadiums – like that of Nacional Medellín FC's – regularly drew crowds of more than 30,000. In those far-off, more innocent days, cocaine cartels were unheard of and the only sharpshooters wore a trim-cut red-and-white-sleeved strip – executioners in Arsenal's colours of Colombia's top football club come from the capital, Bogotá, to outgun the league hopefuls of the outback.

The name of the big city club was Independiente de Santa Fé. And wearing their No. 11 shirt was a short and slightly built Englishman who looked out of place among the array of swarthy Latin giants. But in one short season, this dazzling exponent of raiding wing-play was to become a legend in South American football and a cause célèbre back in his homeland. It was an affair which scandalised English soccer and involved not only one of the game's most dazzling wingers but also a legendary high-society debutante and a millionaire Latino playboy with a diplomatic bag.

Even now, in the early years of the twenty-first century, political turmoil has continued to blight the image of Colombia, but this benighted nation's footballers have never lost the capacity to surprise and delight aficionados of the beautiful game. The national squad has often held its own with the best – including a goalless draw against England in 1995. And in a flamboyantly unpredictable showing in the World Cup campaign of 1998, they lost out to England, despite beating their eventual group winners, Romania. But back in 1950, no one in England would have given Colombia, the archetypal banana republic, a second thought as a footballing nation.

Outlawed from the International Federation of Football

Associations (FIFA) for poaching players from all over the continent, Colombia was a pariah soccer country. That summer, the World Cup finals were taking place in South America, and the prized Jules Rimet trophy was being lifted by Uruguay in a shock upset. But another surprise was on the way. The Colombians had persuaded the new champions of the universe to parade the trophy and their skills in a friendly in Bogotá. It looked set to be a stroll, but what happened has passed into the annals of South American soccer legend – thanks to that Englishman. His name was Charlie Mitten. And when he donned the jersey of the Colombian national team, he became the only player ever capped for three different countries – and the architect of one of the most sensational upsets in soccer history.

It was the first World Cup for more than a decade following the tournament's disruption by the Second World War. And England, who had held aloof from the competition from its inception in 1930, were taking part for the first time and were one of the hot favourites. But, as the record books show, nothing went according to script that fateful summer. There were withdrawals and boycotts, including one by Scotland. And a chaotically organised schedule saw Uruguay qualify without playing a game. Of course, England were, absurdly, knocked out by the US side which only three weeks earlier had been comprehensively demolished by a Manchester United tour party which had swept across America like a prairie bushfire.

In the chaos, the host nation Brazil emerged as the sublimely gifted favourites, playing a totally new and exhilarating style of football that was to take over the world. In that summer of 1950, they had coasted to the final match having scored thirteen goals and conceded only two in their last two games. They needed only a draw against Uruguay to secure the Jules Rimet trophy.

Instead, the underdogs from Montevideo ended up as 2–1

winners before a record crowd of almost 200,000 at the Maracana stadium. In a game uniquely renowned for the playfulness of its hyperbole, the truly unimaginable had happened. Brazil had composed a winning anthem and been declared champions by the state governor before their team had even pulled on their match shirts. Their defeat by Uruguay was seen as a national catastrophe.

But, on the day, tiny Uruguay eventually ran out worthy winners. Once they'd weathered the first-half storm which gave Brazil a 1–0 interval lead, players like Schiaffino and Ghiggia, who scored both Uruguay goals, more than matched the flair of the odds-on favourites.

This, then, was the team that flew into Bogotá to play an exhibition game against a country where a soccer revolution was in the making – and freebooting exponents of the beautiful game could earn real riches that matched even the fabled El Dorado. While the Uruguayans paraded the stars who had humbled Brazil, their opponents' squad was made of unsung Colombians and the pick of those guest players from the two Bogotá teams, Santa Fé and Millonarios.

They included Mitten and another Englishman, George Mountford, at wing-half. These two of England's so-called 'Bogotá Brigade' found themselves in illustrious company guesting for a far-off nation of no-hopers – for the scratch Colombian team also included two young Argentinian exiles, Hector Rial and Alfredo di Stefano.

One unprecedented upset followed another as Uruguay made history twice within a matter of weeks. Having beaten the best team in the world, they lost 3–1 to a country considered among the worst.

It was a game Mitten especially remembered on two counts, as he graphically recalled to me in a series of interviews for this book. Apart from the unexpected victory, it showed how tough South American football was going to be, and, second, he got to play with a soccer genius in the making: Alfredo di

Stefano. In the characteristically forthright language that earned him the career soubriquet 'Cheeky', Mitten vividly recalled the match: 'The Uruguayans were fierce, and spread the blood that day. It was running down our legs by the end of the game. They played like demons and took no prisoners. If you saw the sky, you were flat on your back. But it was a great victory.'

Charlie Mitten didn't get his name on the score sheet that day, but he set up one of two goals scored by Colombia's 24-year-old centre-forward, Alfredo di Stefano. Within a year, di Stefano had joined Real Madrid and went on to become the supreme playmaker of the side which dominated Europe throughout the 1950s – the decade of the Busby Babes.

So what was the pedigree of Charlie Mitten who, at 29, was the senior player in the makeshift Colombian national squad that stepped out against the masters of the world in Bogotá that fateful day 56 years ago?

To anyone under 60, the name Charlie Mitten will probably mean little. But his is truly a name to conjure with. He was an ever-present in the post-war side which established the footballing legend that is Manchester United today. Under Matt Busby, a virtually bankrupt, very average pre-war football team was transformed. But it was supreme ball artists like Mitten who made Busby's dream come true on the field. Busby later rated his 'Cheeky Charlie, master of the precision pass' as United's all-time greatest outside-left.

But in the days before the players' contract revolution, Mitten had walked out on the Old Trafford club to become one of soccer's first globe-trotters, seeking the financial rewards he felt unjustly denied. Players like Mitten were only doing what the most junior league player today takes as a formality: exercising what they believed was their right to sign for another club at the end of a contract. The difference then was that the retain-and-transfer system, under which a player first signed for an English League club, negated any concept of timescale in the contract. Players were tied to their mother club for life, or until their boards deigned to let them go. Asking for a transfer was deemed tantamount to treason. But even if a player bucked the system, where could he go to better himself? All the League clubs had signed up to this twentieth-century form of serfdom for more than 50 years. And, in any case, they had arbitrarily imposed a maximum wage level, too. In 1904, it was £4 a week. By 1949, it had reached the princely sum of £12, after the Players Union had come cap in hand begging for a raise. Most of the top players felt that they were tied to a system which impoverished them and enriched their employers. But then it was, after all, only a game.

The season the Bogotá Bandits quit their clubs had seen record gates – an astounding 41.2 million fans paid at the turnstiles to see their favourite team. Players were being transferred for previously unimaginable fees. In March 1949, for example, Manchester United's own Johnny Morris had transferred to Derby County for £25,000, then a new record. The game seemed awash with cash, but the players saw little of it. Just a year earlier there had even been rumblings of a strike, but for all the Union's good intentions, their efforts came to nothing.

Men like Mitten were the first stars to demand and then actively seek the rewards they felt their drawing power deserved. And Mitten wasn't alone. He said he personally knew of around 60 other top players who felt the same way and were seriously considering taking the path to El Dorado blazed by Neil Franklin. But, unlike them, Mitten decided he had to do something about it – with or without the Union's backing. (Johnny Morris said that in 1951 he and two other players at Derby County had agreed to fly out to Bogotá for the close season – with the blessing of the club.)

Today, as a foreign legion of talent runs glorious riot on football grounds up and down the country – for rewards that seem out of this world – such attitudes seem little short of lunacy. But as Matt Busby's treatment of Mitten on his return shows, these attitudes infected the whole game, even its brightest and best managers. What Mitten wanted in 1950 was no more than his due. Fame and glory, yes; but, as Charlie recalled, honours didn't pay the bills.

In that sense, he was a modern soccer star before his time, one who wanted it all from the beautiful game. He went to Bogotá for a contract which earned him as much in one year as the average player could earn in ten years in those days in the English League. Ultimately, though, he ended up an outcast. When he returned from Bogotá, he was shunned by his old club and frozen out of international honours by the soccer establishment. Charlie's teammate, the live-wire Johnny Morris, had no doubts about Mitten's ability. United's first great inside-right told me he rated Charlie among the eight best wingers in the world that he had seen in more than 60 years of football.

Few now doubt it was England's loss. So who was this 'Cheeky' Charlie? And why did he end up a prophet without honour in his own country? And do his credentials qualify him for inclusion among the immortals in soccer's Hall of Fame?

Charlie Mitten was that unique combination of raider and goal-maker. Even the great Stan Matthews was goal-shy compared to him. In his brief season in Colombia, he hit 24 goals with Bogotá Santa Fé, but long before he forsook England for that year in South America, he had established a reputation as one of the deadliest finishers in the game. In four seasons on the left-wing at Manchester United, between 1945 and 1950, he made 161 League and Cup appearances, scoring 61 goals, including 18 spot-kicks. And on that pre-World Cup finals tour of America in 1950, he had unquestionably been the club's star turn, particularly for his penalty-taking.

But none of these feats was able to save Mitten from the petty-mindedness of the game's *éminences grises*, among whom was Matt Busby. Charlie Mitten never gave vent to his true feelings about the treatment meted out to him on his return from Colombia. At the time, press reports spoke of a perky and suntanned Cheeky Charlie leaving the kangaroo court, which was judge, jury and executioner, grateful at the leniency of his sentence. The joint FA–Football League commission which heard the case fined him £250, docked a notional £300 in wages and bonuses and suspended him for six months. The *Daily Mail* reported that as Mitten left the inquiry he said he thought 'they were very fair and the result was better than I expected'. But he'd have preferred that the fine was doubled and the suspension halved.

In the series of interviews he gave me for this book in 1995, however, he finally ended almost 45 years of heroically stoic discretion. Pressed about his true feelings, Mitten admitted that he thought the whole affair had been 'a bloody disgrace'. (In 2001, just months before his death, he was still complaining that United owed him £250 because they'd had no right to fine him on top of the FA penalty.) He was particularly bitter about being cut dead by Matt Busby, whom he'd always regarded as something of a father figure. Later in life, when he spoke of Busby, there was an ambivalence in his feelings which he never completely lost. But when Matt refused to take him back at United, Mitten's whole world collapsed.

Quite simply, Charlie Mitten's sole aim in life was to play soccer at the highest level, with the best team in the country. It had been his ambition ever since he started out in Scottish junior football. To be deprived of that prize when he considered himself at the height of his powers was a bitter blow. 'I told Matt before the FA inquiry that United were making a big mistake and that I was a better player than I'd ever been. They could give me a month's trial to find out if I was telling the truth. But it was no use. Matt was still the perfect gent he'd always been, but he made it clear the board were making an example of me.'

Not being taken back was bad enough, but not being allowed to train on United's ground was worse – even though, as he admitted in 1995, it had been easy enough to pop round to the local park near his house in Stretford, just half a mile from Old Trafford, to keep fit. 'It was spiteful and vindictive; they were like little children: "You can't play with my ball,"' he told me.

Looking back with the advantage of hindsight on the cutting short of Charlie Mitten's international career in the 1950s, there does seem to have been an uncanny and ironic counterpoint in the gradual demise of England's world supremacy in soccer, culminating in a dismal, no-win run of eight games – four of them in the 1958 World Cup campaign. It was a parallel Mitten was reluctant to entertain. As he always said, he never found it easy to judge his own worth, to regard himself as a top-class footballer on a par with the best of his generation. Certainly, he was never a prima donna, as anyone who ever played with or against him has always testified. Many recalled, for example, the game in which he famously advised a referee trying to book a full-back reluctant to give his name, to buy a match programme. And he got away with it. George McCabe, League official 1952–69, including the 1966 World Cup finals, and later an archivist at Sheffield United, regularly refereed Fulham games when Charlie was at Craven Cottage. He recalled Mitten's banter was always good-natured, never sarcastic. 'Charlie was a bit cocky, always had something to say – but I never had any trouble with him. Those were the days when players could talk to the ref. It's different now.'

Charlie was cheeky, yes. Arrogant, never! 'I always preferred to keep a low profile when I was a player. I liked to let my football do the talking. Adulation didn't mean a thing to me; the very idea still embarrasses me.'

So when he returned from South America, he was naive enough to think that his warnings of the soccer hurricane on the way would be gratefully listened to. Matt Busby, although sceptical initially, took heed and went on to fashion the greatest club side in Britain. The soccer establishment, on the other hand, buried its head in the sand.

This was nothing new. Until the players' contract revolution in 1960, English football, based on a feudal system of labour relations, had consistently disdained the new, the unfamiliar and anything which challenged the monopoly powers of the petits bourgeois who ran the game. Pre-war history is littered with examples: numbered shirts, floodlights and even a white ball for easier visibility were resisted for years. But perhaps the most glaring example was England's refusal to participate in the World Cup throughout the 1930s from its inception. And the English game's obsession with speed, aggression and tactics in the decades after their one-and-only success in 1966 was equally short-sighted, I was told by Mitten, who had one great chance to change things – and failed.

In the immediate post-war years, the smug attitude of supremacy continued, and when England finally deigned to join the rest of the world in 1950, they expected a cakewalk. But the signs that English football was mired in a time warp were there for all to see. In Lisbon in 1947, they had beaten Portugal 10–0, with Blackpool debutant Stan Mortensen and Tommy Lawton – who became the first £20,000 transfer when he moved to Third Division Notts County from Chelsea – scoring four each. But nine days earlier, the national team lost 1–0 to Switzerland in Zurich. Three years later, when Portugal came to Wembley for the return match, only four goals from a breathtaking Tom Finney enabled England to prevail 5–3. A few prescient heads murmured it would not do for South America.

And so it proved. And after their ignominious defeat by the US part-timers, the England tour party didn't even bother staying for the Jules Rimet final game to see at first-hand what was coming. They caught the plane home – as did most of the journalists – and so missed a forewarning of the kind of magic that was to leave England utterly bewitched at Wembley three years later. But Mitten's one season in Colombia was enough to convince him of the football revolution that was on the way: 'I said to Matt as soon as I came back from South America, "Football's going to change, boss. I've seen teams out there who, to a man, can take the lace out of the ball before you get near them. Even the centre-halfs and full-backs can do it." He said, "Any good players?" I said, "Di Stefano and Rial, there's two." Matt was a player himself who liked to beat a man, so he understood. After he saw the Hungarians give us a lesson, he said to me afterwards, "You're right, laddie. We'll have to do something about this." He knew what was happening. He was always a learner.'

The final shot in the players' contract revolution was fired in October 1995 by Jean-Marc Bosman. The European Court of Justice ruled that it was illegal for any European Union club to operate a nationality quota. Charlie Mitten heard the verdict with quiet satisfaction. He had long advocated an end to such restrictions and believed it provided a unique opportunity for the game to make a quantum leap – to total and unfettered mobility of players not only at club but also at country level. Outrageous? Maybe. Revolutionary? Certainly. But in the five years since Mitten's death, many of his visionary ideas have come to pass, with total freedom of movement and players both EU and non-EU even having the option of choosing which national team shirt they'll pull on.

And the spectre which Charlie Mitten believed haunted English football for almost 40 years finally looks to be fading away, although the national team is still trying to recover its pre-eminence in the game it gave the world. At the highest level – the World Cup – England are still also-rans, notwithstanding the remarkable feat of Alf Ramsey's side in 1966. For three decades, 1966 had been a mere blip in the

English game's tardiness in coming to terms with its own shortcomings, thought Mitten. Only over the past five years, perhaps, has a new approach that nurtures technique as much as teamwork, commitment and luck, brought the promise of a brighter future back to the homeland of the beautiful game.

After England's failure in Euro '96 and 2000, and the World Cup in '98, Cheeky Charlie Mitten still reckoned he knew the answers – just as he did all those years ago when few were prepared to listen. After a colourful career in which he became the only player capped by three countries, and the youngest manager in the English League's top division, Mitten reckoned the solution was simplicity itself.

These, then, are the memoirs of a soccer outlaw who, in a life dedicated to the beautiful game, had only one regret – that he turned down Real Madrid.

# 2

# England Expects

We know you are the best outside-left in the country,
Charlie, but we can't select you for England – discipline
comes first.

Stanley Rous, FA secretary

NEMESIS CAME TO ENGLISH SOCCER ON 25 NOVEMBER 1953.
The Hungarian national team strode out at Wembley and
slaughtered England 6–3. The headlines the next day said it
all: the 'Magyar masters' had handed out a lesson, and it was
'Back to school' for England. Six months later, England's
shell-shocked selectors made seven changes for the return
game in Budapest. Hungary won again – this time by a margin
of 7–1, inflicting England's worst-ever defeat in an
international.

It is difficult to overstate the impact of the Hungarians'
demolition of English soccer pretensions. Never before had a
foreign team come to the lion's den and prevailed. (Eire's 2–0
win in the 1949 'home' international was deemed not to count
– and, anyway, nine of the Irish squad were English League
players, including their skipper, Johnny Carey of Manchester
United.) Nothing, not even the 1950 World Cup failure, had

prepared the country's soccer establishment for this humiliation.

'Leaden-footed' was how the press described England, and a reprise of Hungary's most celebrated goal shows that the verdict was far from misplaced. The Magyars went 3–0 up when their captain, Ferenc Puskas, impudently dragged the ball back with the sole of his boot just outside the six-yard box, and left centre-half Billy Wright chasing shadows. (There'd been a forewarning six months earlier when Uruguay completely bewitched England 2–1 in Montevideo, in a dazzling exhibition which could easily have ended 6–1 to the South Americans. In one of the game's most astonishing pieces of trickery, centre-forward Miguez left Wright rooted to the spot as he flipped the ball over the England man, darted round him and caught the ball on his head.) As the England captain, supposedly the unshakeable rock in defence, later admitted of Puskas's goal: 'As I made the challenge, he pulled the ball back like a man loading a shotgun and fired it into the net while I was tackling thin air.'

It was not that England played particularly badly. What was really disturbing was the huge gulf in basic technical ability which the Hungarians mercilessly exposed. Even the legendary Stan Matthews was upstaged, although, at 38, he could perhaps be forgiven for being unable to fire England. Charlie Mitten watched the match and later remembered the sublime exhibition of skill which tore England apart: 'It was like a lesson, with teachers and schoolboys. The England team looked like Manchester United and Blackburn Rovers did in the 1995 European Champions League – the gap in individual skills was so great. There were "ooohs" and "aaahs" every time a Hungarian touched the ball – any Hungarian. You wouldn't believe it. Even defenders were pushing the ball forward and setting up attacks for Puskas and Co. The England players were deathly quiet as they came off the pitch at the end of the game. That should have been the turning point. The FA should have said, "Come on, they've caught us out, what's happened?" and looked to the future.'

The English team that bleak November day was without two of its best players. Neither was injured, and both were tried and tested in the cauldron of international soccer. One was centre-half Neil Franklin, winner of 37 consecutive post-war caps. He was a totally new kind of central defender – one who could play the ball as well as stop the man. The other was Mitten, who had played for England just once, in 1946. But neither was ever to win international honours again. Indeed, the FA had changed centre-halfs no fewer than ten times rather than recall Franklin. Mitten, too, was ignored despite a series of devastating displays for Fulham on his return from Bogotá. They were *personae non gratae* to the selectors because they'd defected to Colombia.

Franklin was unarguably the most sophisticated and skilful centre-half of his era, perhaps the best that England has ever had, and Mitten's unquestioned fast goal-raiding ability, honed at Manchester United, had been anointed with South American flair on the ball during his season abroad. Could these two men have made a difference? Charlie Mitten would never have claimed that himself. But he did vividly recall that he'd seen it all coming at first hand.

But even with Mitten and Franklin on the field, would England really have fared any better against the Hungarians that day? Two men, as Mitten freely admitted, didn't make a great team. It was too easy to react to the brilliance of individual players without assessing how they fitted into the sub-group structures of their club side.

'If you look back and say, "Well, how did this happen, how did he get the ball to do it, who won the tackle, who made the pass?" and you say, "They're good players, too," you assess them as a little group working in the team. Perhaps there should be more consideration of little groups of players – twos and threes – players who know each other and work well together at their club. I look back on my career and think of that United side of 1950. We finished fourth, three points behind the champions Portsmouth, and were runners-up the previous three seasons. I can honestly say that, at Wembley in 1953, it could have been me there against the Hungarians, with Henry Cockburn behind, Stan Pearson inside and Jack Rowley playing at centre-forward. We were doing it at club level week after week, against the same people who were turning out for Ireland, Scotland and Wales in internationals, and making monkeys out of them. The only monkeys we couldn't make were the England selectors.'

Neil Franklin had the kind of skills they took for granted in South America, and the Continentals adapted this approach. 'It was South American flair that was polished at Wembley that day, and those skills were murderous. The contrast couldn't have been greater between the top-class technical ability which every man in the Hungarian side had, and which with obvious exceptions was lacking in the England team. Everyone talks about collective team spirit, that you can't beat the strength of a well-drilled team. But give me only three lads who can manipulate a ball and I'll make inroads into any team in the world, no matter how well organised,' Charlie said.

Mitten insisted that what crept into English football in the 1950s was a nervous fear among players, especially attackers, about losing the ball, getting beaten by the opposing player. Speaking in 1996, he told me his belief that English soccer was still in thrall to that demon. But where did it come from? Mitten was convinced it emanated from those who directed the game at the top, from the international side down, and it was an approach emulated by coaches, trainers and managers down to the most junior level. As we shall see, Mitten believed football was still caught in the dead-end trap of physicality and aggression, which went a long way to explaining the failure of England in the World Cup since 1966 (and, one might say, of English clubs in Europe for most of the 1990s). He thought

Terry Venables did a good job in difficult circumstances and that the same fundamental problem faced Glenn Hoddle: the lack of world-class flair and talent. 'Hoddle was a great player but he will also find he's hunting in a bazaar for quality players that are not there. The best footballers in Britain are foreigners,' he told me in 1996. (Charlie didn't live to see the newest generation of home-grown players coming through the ranks, but he would certainly have enthused over the abundance of technically-gifted players now available to the latest national manager, Sven-Göran Eriksson.)

In 1951, when Charlie Mitten returned from Colombia, nothing could have been further from the minds of the football authorities. Considerations about technical skills were overlooked and conformity was rewarded over merit. Incredibly, those charged with selecting the England squad made no secret of it: they were out to make an example of prodigals.

The game was run as the personal fiefdom of what Jimmy Greaves has described as 'a bunch of retired butchers, bakers and candlestick-makers'. The selection process was nothing personal: others, who recoiled from the kind of drastic steps taken by the Bogotá Bandits, received the same treatment as them if they exhibited too much of an independent spirit. The most celebrated example, perhaps, was Sunderland's Len Shackleton. The so-called 'Clown Prince of Soccer' not only loved scoring goals but also thought that playing football should be fun. Yet his prodigious skills in 320 league appearances for Sunderland brought only five caps. Shack didn't give a fig for the Buggins's-turn bigwigs who ran the game; he was too much of an individualist. For his debut international against Denmark in Copenhagen, which ended in a goalless draw, he wore rugby boots, which he said were more comfortable; in his last appearance for his country, his cheeky chip shot over the advancing goalkeeper clinched a 3–1 win over West Germany at Wembley. He was nothing if not an entertainer, and the fans loved it.

Cheeky Charlie, too, made clowns out of the game's rulers, and they never forgave him either. Mitten was never capped again – whether or not England needed him. Few doubt that it was because he stepped out of line and defied the game's establishment. He was the most talented of the exiles who dared to seek the rewards they felt they merited without the blessing of the clubs or the FA.

Indeed, FA chief Sir Stanley Rous, who later became president of FIFA, admitted as much. As the *United Review* has recorded, he once told the winger, after a particularly scintillating Fulham performance, 'We know you're the best outside-left in the country, Charlie, but we can't select you for England – discipline must come first.'

That such blind prejudice was allowed to get in the way of forging a team capable of defending England's reputation against the world seems incredible today. Certainly, it was no part of England manager Walter Winterbottom's calculations. He had been a Manchester United player, and during the war had been Charlie Mitten's boss as the RAF's head of physical training. The FA appointed him England's first manager in 1946, but the real power remained with the amateurs on the selection committee. He was effectively shackled by the petty regional rivalries, personal jealousies and pet-player partisanship of the selectors who were, of course, made up of club chairmen.

This club-before-country attitude was to persist well into the 1960s. Winterbottom was lucky if he got the same team two games running, and even luckier if they arrived at the England training camp more than 24 hours before kick-off for a get-together. To expect a team to be selected on some coherent basis of merit and strategy was like wishing for the moon. The players themselves understood very well what was going on. As Charlie recalled: 'You'd get a dozen chairmen around the table in that FA committee and each one would only be interested in looking after his own club. There'd be a dozen different votes on each player, and they'd be horse-trading – "my lad this time, yours next". Being an international increased a player's worth in transfer fees.'

Given such a set-up, when Mitten followed Stoke City's Neil Franklin on the road to Colombia in 1950, they were signing their own international death warrants – although Mitten certainly didn't think so at the time. He felt he was perfectly within his rights. So just what was the heinous crime which Mitten, Franklin, George Mountford and Billy Higgins (of Everton) and Bobby Flavell (of Motherwell) committed? And what were the circumstances which provoked them into such drastic action?

The flight to Bogotá had its roots in the failure of the Players Union to mount a serious challenge to the autocratic hegemony which the League sought to maintain over football in the immediate post-war period. The Players Union had been formed in 1907 and the driving force behind it was Billy Meredith. More than 500 players had attended the inaugural meeting at the Imperial Hotel in Manchester to demand an increase in the maximum wage of £4 a week together with freedom of contract. Meredith was the eccentric Welsh international goal-scoring wing genius who propelled Manchester United to greatness in the early years of the twentieth century. He'd been a Manchester City player until 1903, when he was banned from the club *sine die* after admitting accepting illicit payments in a bribery and bung scandal for which he was made the scapegoat. Sound familiar? He was snapped up by United, but his experience turned him into a bitter critic of the system which he spent the rest of his playing career – and life – fighting. The union he helped found was the chief vehicle of this struggle, but he was not to live to see its eventual triumph. He died in 1957.

The 1939–45 war had robbed many professional footballers of the best years of their career. And when the full league programme resumed in 1946, an entertainment-starved populace, faced with years of rationing austerity, flocked to grounds all over the country in an explosion of enthusiasm for the game. Gates regularly soared to 70,000-plus. (Indeed, midweek games were banned following an FA Cup semi-final tie between Derby County and Birmingham at Maine Road which attracted more than 80,000 spectators; the government feared the effect of factory absenteeism on post-war reconstruction efforts.) Clubs seemed to have bottomless bank accounts as transfer fees rocketed. With the players' wage bill at even the most well-endowed club running to perhaps £300 a week (30 professionals at an average £10 a week), and gate income averaging perhaps £5,000 (50,000 fans at two bob – 10p), League pleas of poverty seemed at best unconvincing. In 1948, for example, Everton had posted profits of £25,000, Spurs £20,000, Burnley £19,000 and Manchester City £16,000 – enormous sums if scaled up to today's equivalents.

In a new mood of militancy, a tough new leadership of the Players Union under Jimmy Guthrie demanded a share of the spoils – a higher maximum wage as well as a new contract system and a provident fund. But the Players Union was outmanoeuvred by League negotiations over two seasons of strike-threat brinkmanship, and when a settlement was finally hammered out under the auspices of the new Labour government's compulsory National Arbitration Tribunal, the Union settled for a new full-time players' maximum of £12 (£10 in summer) and a new £7 minimum (£5 in summer). And the £12 was very much the maximum: the vast majority of players got far less. In 1949, two years of negotiations over a generous new provident fund retirement pay-out scheme to replace the grace-and-favour system of players' benefits, ended in a vastly inferior League-proposed scheme. It was, however, better than nothing.

But there was no progress on the substantive question of the retain-and-transfer system. The League refused even to discuss it, although the tribunal, while making no formal recommendation, suggested a joint negotiating committee along the lines of the Whitley Councils which oversaw other industries. It was this system which kept players in thrall to their club paymasters, and – officially – prevented the specially talented individual from securing any reward greater than the maximum wage paid to any other player, despite his drawing power at the turnstiles.

The system worked like this: when a player signed professional forms for a club at the age of 17, he was deemed – by the clubs acting collectively as the League – tied for as long as that club wished, irrespective of whether he was out of contract. The system grew out of the FA's concern to control professionals during the amateur–professional split at the inception of the League more than a hundred years ago. A professional player was required to register annually or he wouldn't be allowed to play, and he couldn't change clubs in mid-season without the FA's permission.

The League seized on this to corner the market in their most precious commodity – manpower. The clubs agreed among themselves that once a player had signed, he had to obtain the permission of his club if he wished to move – and that no player, no matter what his status, could be paid any more than a fixed maximum wage. The League justified these unique arrangements, which reduced a player to a bonded chattel, as being in the mutual interests of all clubs – to prevent the poaching of 'greedy' star players from small clubs by richer clubs. Where a player was allowed to go, the transfer-fee system meant that compensation for the 'selling' club was agreed before the player could register and thus play for his new club. Obviously, under this rubric, a player who refused to sign a new contract for the new season couldn't play – or earn a living.

At the heart of these arrangements was the technical question of *what* was being bought: it was not the *player*, but his *registration*, said the League. And it was on this distinction that the legal challenges to the system by the Players Union were based over the years – all unsuccessfully conducted until the Eastham case came to court in 1963.

All this might not have mattered if the players had felt they were dealing with good-willed, even paternalistic employers, but too many clubs treated their players like serfs. In the atmosphere of post-war turmoil, the iniquities of the system became especially galling to players like Mitten. He felt he was reaching the peak of his career but had no obvious prospects of building for the future after his all-too-brief playing career was over.

Despite the maximum which the top stars could earn, most players got less and many could hardly make ends meet, as was highlighted by a largely sympathetic press. Alan Hoby, fulminating in *The People* against the 'League Führers', claimed that 'behind the glamour of the world's greatest game and the cascades of cash bursting in the tills of League clubs was a seamier side to an entertainment industry which still ranked among the poorest paid on earth'.

Charlie Mitten was among the elite, playing for a club that between 1946 and 1949 posted profits of just under £100,000, yet he, too, could hardly make ends meet. He was one of United's most reliable performers, and had a wife and three young children to support. Yet the club were only paying him £10 a week basic – and clawing back £1 10 shillings (£1.50) in rent for his club-owned house. It didn't look like a fair trade-off to Mitten: 'At United, we'd won just about everything that English football had to offer – League runners-up three seasons in a row and FA Cup winners in 1948, and yet we had nothing! Getting to the Cup final was a big bonus for players, but even then, you only got £20 for winning the Cup – and nothing for losing! And there was £9 in tax off that! Even the band got more than the players for appearing at Wembley. But they probably played better.'

It was vintage Cheeky Charlie. He was joking, of course –

but only about the band playing better. The mirth masked the great wellspring of discontent felt by players of that era even among star teams like United. Indeed, it actually led to a mutiny at Old Trafford on the eve of the 1948 Cup final.

One of the big annual perks for players was their allocation of Cup final tickets. Given their restricted wages at that time, these tickets also represented a significant financial bonus, as many players sold their allocation on or even exchanged them for goods in kind. But, only weeks before the final, the club announced that the number of players' tickets was to be cut from 100 to 12. The effect in the United dressing-room was electric, as Charlie recalled: 'We said, "Bloody hell, we've all got more relatives than that." And, of course, everybody wanted to make a bit of cash from selling some of their tickets. So we had meetings with Matt Busby, and told him, "Boss, we're not happy about this; we're not going to play." Matt's first reaction was anger – he said he'd turn out the reserves. So we said, "Go ahead, let them play." He didn't, of course. He got round it, somehow, and we all got our 100 tickets each.'

Clearly, coveting honours offended no one: the unforgivable sin was expecting to be rewarded handsomely for achieving them.

'The flight to Bogotá was a blazing symbol of what was going on in the minds of professional footballers throughout the country. The cash terms being offered by these foreign clubs was a huge inducement. The press started to take notice. For the first time, people began to realise the worth of a top professional footballer in terms of hard cash, entertainment value and drawing power to his club.'

It was a brave and understandable gamble, but it certainly wasn't recklessness. Mitten was convinced that he had the law on his side when he set off for South America, despite the legacy of the Kingaby case. In that 1912 court ruling, the Union lost an action brought on behalf of Aston Villa's 24-year-old winger, Herbert Kingaby, an unlikely star at 5 ft 7 in.

who weighed less than 11 st. But his fast and aggressive wing-play earned him the nickname of 'The Rabbit' as well as the attention of other clubs. He had been kept out of football for two years after seeking a transfer because the club had posted a ludicrously high fee for his signature. But what looked like a promising case in law was bungled when union lawyers focused on the club's motives – accusing it of malice rather than questioning the legality of the system itself. It was a disaster for the players and the Union, which was virtually bankrupted by the legal costs. The setback undermined players' confidence in the Union, which thereafter was reluctant to go to law again.

But, in 1950, it was precisely on the contract issue that Mitten had sought counsel's opinion, and he'd been advised that he had what looked like a watertight case in law. But Charlie felt unable to take the huge financial risk of what would have been a vigorously defended lawsuit. Emboldened by his legal advice – namely that refusing to sign a new contract with Manchester United left him a free agent to sell his labour where he chose – Mitten struck out for El Dorado.

'I thought that, at twenty-nine years of age, I could expect at the most five or six more seasons in the First Division, and then I'd find myself back where I started as a seventeen year old – with no money in the bank, a wife and children to support and looking around for another living. The most I'd ever earned as a professional footballer had been £10 a week, and there seemed nothing I could do to provide my family with security. I was well aware that not every ex-player could be a manger or hold an official position off the field of play. I'd been at the top of the tree with United, and all I had to show for my career to date was an old second-hand car.'

If things didn't work out, Charlie fully expected to be able to return to club and country with no hard feelings on either side. After all, even before he'd refined his devastating wing-raiding at United, his skills had been sought by England and Scotland – both countries had actually picked him for internationals. It never made the record books, and to discover why, and how it happened, we have to go back to first beginnings in the life of the Bogotá Bandit.

# 3

# Dirky Dancing

You see that player, son? He's the kind who sets things happening!

Matt Busby on Stanley Matthews, 1938

CHARLIE MITTEN PLAYED HIS FIRST AND ONLY GAME FOR England at the age of 25 when he was selected against Scotland for the Bolton Disaster Fund match of 1946. The game didn't qualify for a national honours cap, although it was certainly a full international in everything but name. Mitten played outside-left in the match at Manchester City's old Maine Road ground in a line-up that included Stan Matthews, Billy Wright, Tommy Lawton and Frank Swift, with Wilf Mannion on the bench.

Two years earlier, Mitten had been capped by the Scottish FA as a reserve in a wartime international game against England. Charlie admitted that the Scottish honour came as a big surprise. The selectors had been assured that Charlie's father, then serving as a warrant officer in the Royal Scots regiment, was a true-born Scot. In the confusion of the wartime period, a detailed check was not a priority and, anyway, the records showed that the young Mitten had been a schoolboy in Perthshire before the war and had played in Scottish junior football.

The oddity of Mitten's international record has been matched by few other players. One, Stan Mortensen, England's '12th man', came on as substitute for Wales in a match against England at Wembley in September 1943 to replace the injured Ivor Powell. Wales had been unable to field a reserve in the wartime friendly. Another, Billy Walsh, who was Manchester City's immediate post-war wing-half, played for the Republic of Ireland after being capped by England as a schoolboy.

The Bolton fund match had been organised to help the victims of one of the worst football disasters in the history of the game. It happened at Burnden Park – original home of Bolton Wanderers until their move to the Reebok Stadium – on 9 March 1946; the occasion was the second round of the post-war FA Cup competition which was played on a home and away basis. Bolton had won the first leg 2–0, and the return match at Burnden Park attracted massive crowds eager to see if Stoke could turn the tie around with the help of the incomparable Stanley Matthews, then unquestionably the most illustrious footballer in England.

The official figures put the attendance at 65,000, which was the number recorded when the turnstiles closed. But outside the stadium an estimated 20,000 fans, who found themselves locked out, began gatecrashing the ground. Just before the match started, several terracing barriers collapsed and, in a horrific pile-up, within the space of a few yards, 33 fans were crushed to death and more than 400 injured.

The injured and dying were being treated on the touchline as the game kicked off, most people in the ground unaware that anything untoward had happened. The referee briefly stopped the match but was advised to continue the game for fear of sparking panic – or a riot. (There was a food store under the stands and, with rationing in full force, the police considered the store a greater priority than controlling the gatecrashing fans.) The match, played without a half-time break, ended in a goalless draw. A Home Office inquiry following the disaster called for stricter safety standards at grounds, but its findings were largely ignored.

The massive crowds of the Bolton v. Stoke game were repeated at First Division grounds across the country as entertainment-hungry fans flocked to the exhilarating spectacle of the resumed soccer programme. The only wonder was that there weren't more tragedies. In our modern era of all-seater stadiums, it's hard to believe that Manchester City's old Maine Road ground – now recently demolished after the club's move to Eastlands – regularly packed in 85,000-plus fans, mostly standing on the terraces.

Certainly, with the huge gate receipts which the crowds brought, it was no wonder that clubs were soon breaking the transfer-fee record on an almost monthly basis.

These, then, were the tragic circumstances which led to Charlie Mitten winning his first and only England call-up in 1946. Both the English and Scottish Football Associations had sought his services on the left-wing for the disaster fund match. It was then that more thorough checks revealed that Perthshire had been the adopted home of the Mitten family, and that Mitten Senior, while with a Scottish regiment, had been born a Londoner. The rules were clear: a player took the nationality of his father, thus ending Charlie's international career for Scotland.

Not that his sole England appearance was particularly auspicious, despite an adulatory build-up in the press. The *Evening Chronicle* reported: 'Mitten may become one of the greatest outside-lefts England has ever had.' Always fearlessly self-critical, looking back, Charlie felt he wasn't ready for the challenge: 'I didn't have a good game. I think they may have picked me because the match was in Manchester and, of course, having Manchester club players got interest going among the crowd. I was a very popular player on the terraces [at Maine Road, where United played all their home games until 1950]. They used to sing "Charlie is My Darling" when I scored for United. But I felt a total stranger in that match. I didn't know my inside-forward or half-back. I was just pitched in. It does make a difference – you've got to know your partners inside out. I realised then that international games are totally different from league matches.'

But reports of the match indicated that the fault was certainly not all Mitten's. One account identified not lack of skill, but lack of understanding between Mitten and Australian-born left-half Frank Mitchell and Everton inside-left Wally Fielding. Henry Rose in the *Daily Express* wrote: 'Because of an inexplicably weak display by Mitchell, Mitten was pass-starved and Fielding was inclined to work the ball too much to the centre or the right wing . . . But because no player should be judged on a single showing, I would give a further chance to the Fielding–Mitten left-wing.'

Rose was discussing the possible team for the forthcoming full international against Northern Ireland, and his analysis struck a chord with Charlie. He felt that this was maybe a mistake England made throughout the 1990s, especially given the domestic predominance of Manchester United: 'No individual can get to know how his wing-half or inside men play in three weeks. If an international manager is going to select a new individual player, he should consider playing him for at least half a dozen consecutive matches, because it takes that long for players to get to know each other. And, in his first game for the national honours there's the added pressure that, if he doesn't play well, he won't get picked again. There's always that feeling at the back of your mind that you're playing in a one-off match and that you daren't try this, daren't do that. That's how I felt.

'I remember during the tactics talk with Walter Winterbottom at Buxton before the game. He said, "Charlie,

I know you like the ball and to beat the man and that, but just get them nicely across, son." So I said, "OK, Walter, when I get up to the corner flag, and the full-back's on the goal side of me, I'll give you a shout." He says, "What do you mean?" And I said, "Well, you're telling me not to beat him, and I can't get the ball across because he's standing in front of me – so what am I going to do with the bloody thing?" He just turned and walked away.

'When he came to Stan Matthews, he never said a word except, "Do your stuff, Stan." I was the new boy. Stan was the established star and had done it all before. I knew I could turn it on just like Stan, and they knew it – of course they did! But it was all tactical nonsense – instead of saying to me, "Look, Charlie, do what you do at United, because we picked you for playing that way. Get on and do it! If you can take them on at United, you can take them on anywhere in the world."'

And so it was to prove. But then Charlie Mitten had been born a child of the world. His birthplace was neither England nor Scotland – but Rangoon, capital of what was then Burma (now Myanmar), on 17 January 1921. He was the eldest of four children of John Mitten, a career serviceman and physical training instructor, and his wife, Mary. He had one sister, Betty, and two brothers, Sam and John, who were all born in Bombay when his father was posted there. Betty later married a Canadian soldier and went to live in North Bay, Ontario.

Perhaps not surprisingly, Charlie's brothers were good footballers too. They both played for Ballymena in the Irish League, and the younger, John, played at outside-right for a League of Ireland representative side against the Football League. He was a heavy smoker, however, and died of cancer. Neither had the total love of the game essential for any player to scale the heights, but Charlie had no doubt that if they had taken it up seriously, they could have made the grade.

He himself fell hopelessly and utterly in love with the game when he started at school at the age of seven: 'At Christmas, all I ever wanted was a football and a pair of football boots.' As he was later to write when he took over the management of Newcastle United: 'Association football has given me a great life. I love soccer. I always have. Even today, as I set about my daily duties managing one of the greatest football clubs in England, nothing gives me greater happiness than the thought that my own two sons, John and Charlie Junior, are as crazily mad on the game as their father.'

In 1929, Charlie's father, a company sergeant-major in the Royal Scots, was transferred back to his regimental base in Glasgow, and the family came home from India, settling in Scotland. Shortly afterwards, Charlie's father retired from the Army and took a job as physical training instructor at the Queen Victoria Military School at Dunblane in Perthshire. Charlie was seven and went on to complete all his schooling in Scotland. Even in his later years as an adopted Mancunian, his voice never lost the traces of the soft Scots burr he acquired in his formative years.

As a soccer-mad schoolboy, Arsenal were Charlie's favourite team. It was the early 1930s, and the north London club had been transformed under the inspirational leadership of Herbert Chapman. In 1930, Arsenal had won the FA Cup, and the following season they dominated the First Division from the outset, cruising to the first league championship ever won by a southern club. Far away, north of the border, young Master Mitten dreamed of playing for the illustrious Gunners.

The family home was a schoolhouse on the Queen Victoria compound at Dunblane, and every day after school, the young Mitten would pull on his boots and be out kicking a football against the gable end of the row, preparing to make that dream come true. Hour after hour, night after night, until it was too dark to see, the ball would be fired at the wall. He'd mark little spots on the wall and practise hitting them from further and further back. Boom! Boom! Boom! Quite unconsciously, young Charlie was developing innate skills, though, he laughingly admitted, it used to drive his mum to distraction.

Looking back at the wide choice of activities at what was a very games-orientated school, Charlie recalled that he could so easily have taken up another sport or profession: 'Life can so easily take the unexpected course. It would not have been surprising if I had made the Army my career, or if rugby had been my sport. The principal game at Queen Victoria was rugger, and I played rugby league for the school as well as soccer. There was every sport you could think of, including boxing. My father was a good boxer and once fought Jim Driscoll in an Army exhibition bout when he was champion. I grew up at a school that was a paradise – you did your academic studies, then learned military skills, reading the compass, shooting, and we had all these games.'

The young Mitten excelled at athletics, too, and was the school victor ludorum. In the rugby team, he would take the kicks because he was found to have the hardest and most accurate shot, and the young Mitten honed the key skill of long-range accuracy with an elliptical ball! He could never have guessed how invaluable it would prove. As for the other rugger skills, he admitted that in those days he couldn't run very fast with the ball. 'I fancied football better – there seemed to be more you could do with the ball; rugby was a passing game, all rush and tackling. I thought, I'm going to lose my teeth here.'

By the time he was 13, he was playing representative soccer for his school, and it was now that others first spotted his talent. The local junior team, Strathallan Hawthorn at Bridge of Allan near Stirling, asked his father if Charlie could turn out for them in the local league. He was 14 when, at 5 ft nothing and whippet-thin, he made his competitive debut. Many of the opposing players were very much bigger, but Charlie Mitten was faster and had the uncanny knack of being able to ghost clear of trouble or, at worst, ride the fiercest tackle without getting hurt. And to his dying day, he put his special agility down to sword dancing.

At Queen Victoria, the bagpipes, Highland reels and sword dancing were an integral part of the school's rich and varied curriculum. All the boys did it. Young Mitten even played in the pipe band at Murrayfield for the England rugby international. Today, the school still provides the band and the young piper for Scotland's home international rugby matches. He recalled how it paid off later: 'At the time, I was proud to see myself as a Highland laddie. I only realised how important the sword dancing was much later, when I analysed what I was doing. I thought, why do they keep saying to me, "You skip round the full-back, and he just misses you."? I thought, they're not *just* missing me – I'm *doing* it so they miss me! Even Matt Busby would say to me at half-time, "Charlie, this full-back, he only *just* missed you, son!" And I'd say, "That's right, boss, he *just* missed me, because I came away with the ball and made damn sure he did *just* miss me!"'

So what has all this to do with two crossed claymores on the ground? Mitten, a trained physical instructor, always insisted that Highland dancing was the perfect exercise for developing muscle tone, balance and agility – invaluable assets to any athlete. It is anything but a 'soft, sissy' activity, as any Highland or, indeed, classical ballet dancer will tell you. Mitten regarded it as the single most important physical activity that contributed to his footballing ability. He could still do it well into his 70s, and would delight in giving you an impromptu demonstration in the kitchen of his Stockport flat when you visited him.

He recalled: 'Sword dancing is a magnificent exercise that can benefit all athletes. It's the most perfect physical exercise for footballing skills, because you've got to control something with your feet while doing the athletic things like running and jumping, turning and twisting. You instinctively know where to put your feet – your balance has to be correct when you're skipping over obstacles like a couple of sharp, crossed swords. It makes you nimble, all right, and exercises the leg muscles, especially the calves. It enables you to jump nimbly and change direction in the air, anywhere. I would say sword dancing and country dancing were the most important exercises I've found to help me in my football skills. It helped me in my quickness. I could get into my stride quicker, turn in those tight spaces – you're twirling and twisting and you've still got your balance.

'The balance required for Highland dancing is total. And a footballer has got to have balance. This is the key, innate need: balance. How can you go round a man with the ball? What's the key thing you need to do that, physically? Total control over your centre of gravity. I'd often come off the field at United and I'd never have a mark on my shorts – because of my balance. I might have been tripped, but I never fell or slipped. They used to say to me, "We don't need to wash your shorts, Charlie, you can wear them again next week."'

For years afterwards, Highland dancing remained the big secret of Mitten's footballing skill. The connotations in those days with 'sissyness' made him reluctant to disclose the part it had played in his development. But a generation of full-backs whom he left for dead knew to their cost that Charlie Mitten had an uncanny talent for keeping out of trouble.

Years later, when in charge at Newcastle, he finally got the chance to put his theories into practice. The Magpies had some of the most cultured ball-artists in the world on their books, but the outcome, as we shall see, was totally unexpected.

Back in 1935, it was defences in Scottish junior football who were being given the run-around. With his speed off the mark and ball control, the young Charlie started scoring goals. There were obviously off-days, and he remembered with affection how his father would conduct detailed post-mortems on his every performance around the tea table at home in the evening after matches.

'I liked to score, but I never gave it a thought; I'd say to my dad afterwards, "I enjoyed that." But he was very keen on what I did wrong as well as what I did right. He and my mother would watch every match I played for the school and the Hawthorns, and afterwards he'd give me a digest of my mistakes and always have the antidotes. "This is what you should have done, and this is what you did; this is what you did, which was wrong, this is what you could have done." He encouraged me all the time. This is very important for a youngster. At junior level, you need a dad or someone encouraging you all the time. It's a stepping stone, a first rung up the ladder – it's this influence which says you're either going up or staying down. My mum never let on, though she was secretly very proud of me.'

Within a year, Manchester United's brilliantly tuned scouting network in Scotland had picked up on a star in the making, and recommended Charlie to Scott Duncan, United's boss. Mitten Senior agreed that his son should go to Old Trafford for trials and, if good enough, take up a football career rather than go to Army Cadet school at Sandhurst as planned. Within a month, Charlie Mitten was on the ground staff in Manchester. 'My dad had been a soldier all his life, but he didn't make me follow him. He knew I wanted to play football, and so the choice was my own. He gave me the options. I said, "Yes, I'll have a go." He thought I had the ability to be a good footballer. He was quite a good judge. He must have realised I had potential, so he took a chance.'

There were other clubs, of course, who'd had reports of this wing wizard in the making, most notably Rangers, who had also invited him for a trial. But as Charlie recalled it, 'there did not seem to be a lot of push for youngsters in Scotland in those days'.

So, in the absence of a direct approach from Highbury, Charlie took the train for Manchester. And while United were a big-city team, there was no hint of what they were to become. In the 1930s, they were an average English League side, very much overshadowed by their far more successful neighbours, Manchester City. In the words of an old music-hall joke, the club was regarded as 'too good for the Second Division, not good enough for the First' – a sentiment not lost on the young Charlie when he first trooped into the dilapidated Old Trafford ground.

'When I joined the ground staff at United in the June of 1936, the club had just been promoted from the Second Division. But I'd really wanted to go to Arsenal; they were my favourite team at the time. They were big and glamorous and always in the newspapers. I thought, "They're the top team – who are Manchester United? No one's ever heard of them!" But I wanted to play football, and here I was, being welcomed by a club who wanted to give me a chance. One of the first people I got to know at Old Trafford was their talent scout, Louis Rocca, who probably discovered more star footballers than any other man of his time. There was something about the club at that time, although I never imagined what it was going to become.'

That something was the beginnings of the club's first youth policy set up by chairman J.W. Gibson and secretary Walter Crickmer, who had also become caretaker manager after the resignation of Scott Duncan. The Manchester United Junior Athletic Club (MUJAC) programme was to start paying off in the 1938–39 season just before the outbreak of war. The first team finished only 14th in the First division, but the reserves won the Central League, and the A team, helped by a committee of local teachers and coaches from Manchester Unversity, romped through the open-aged Chorlton Amateur League, scoring 223 goals. Chairman Gibson commented that the club did not own the young players. 'We only tell them that we hope that if, as a result of what the club has done, they rise to anything like fame, they will bear the club in mind.' These were to prove prophetic words.

Charlie joined at the same time as several other youngsters who would go on with him to make up the post-war team that was to establish the United legend. Among them were Johnny Hanlon, Reuben Scott, Johnny Carey and a Salford lad named Stan Pearson. Charlie, the youngest, acted as office boy as well as helping out around the ground and with the kit and other chores. Walter Winterbottom was at the club at the time, and Charlie recalled having to clean the future England manager's boots. He also remembered his first digs in Stretford, staying with a Mrs Elliott, where he shared lodgings with inside-right Jack Wassall. All became firm friends.

Charlie always had particularly fond memories of trainer Tom Curry, who was to be among the victims of the 1958 Munich air tragedy. A father figure to the youngsters, he was always ready with a kindly word and practical help if there was sickness or domestic trouble at home. He was astute enough to good-humouredly tolerate an occasional explosion of mischief among his high-spirited charges. Always ready to take a leg-pull himself, he would invariably have the last laugh by turning the cold water hosepipe on United's future stars – although he could only have half-guessed how they would turn out.

Charlie had similarly fond memories of second-team manager Bill Inglis. His indulgence was often rewarded with the 'Vanishing Third-Team Trick'. All the ground staff lads would skive off and hide, to dodge sweeping up or other chores at the ground. Charlie always smiled when he recalled a nonplussed Bill Inglis wondering why he could never find his young scallywags – who, as often as not, would be secreted en masse in a hidden corner beneath the stands engaged in a hectic session of halfpenny brag. It was a camaraderie that was to distil into the invincible team spirit which has always been part of United's most successful sides.

'Right up to the outbreak of war, we were always together on and off duty. We all played in the A team. Johnny Carey was the last to join us just before the war; he came as an inside-

56

forward. A big, gangling, farmer's boy, Johnny found the game a bit too quick for him in those days when he was playing up front. But Matt turned him into one of the best right-backs in the game. My particular pal was inside-left Stan Pearson, and we ended up playing most of our careers alongside each other. Stan and I developed a fine understanding on the left-wing. Each came to instinctively know what the other was going to do with the ball, and we began to make a permanent niche for ourselves as a left-wing pair.'

Of course, as well as coaching and training, there was also the chance to watch top soccer stars of the day in action at internationals in Manchester. And it was a display by Stanley Matthews which proved to be an important influence on the young Mitten's game. Charlie was in the stands at Maine Road in November 1938 when England beat Northern Ireland 7–0, with Spurs' Willie Hall scoring five to equal the English record. But it was Matthews' game – he was unplayable. A legend was being born. At the time, Matthews had been in dispute with Stoke and had asked for a transfer. In the Potteries, thousands marched in protest against the club's decision, and the Wizard of Dribble, who had joined the Stoke ground staff at 15 on £1 a week, stayed.

'It was the first time I'd had the chance to see Stan close-up in a match. He had a great game; he even scored a goal. He had that one trick – a shimmy, inside to the left, then outside with the right foot. His body would go one way and the full-back with the swerve, and suddenly Stan's feet would go the other, and he was gone. It didn't look as if he was running at all – but over the first ten yards he was lightning. He did it all over the world. I began to copy Stan's trick – but on the left-wing, inside with the left, outside with the left, and then go. But I also liked to put it through their legs, especially if the defender had managed to get close to me. It wasn't being cheeky, as they said, but the tactical thing to do; it was the only space to get the ball past him.

'What I also remember about the game was that it was the first time I came across Matt Busby. After the match, he said to me, as we were leaving the ground, "You see that player, son? He's the kind who sets things happening!" He was right, of course. But I realised as I got older that Stan must have had good players around him, giving him the service as well. You've got to have "workmen" giving the star the ball, and the star's got to deliver – or he ain't a star.'

As United's A team swept all before them in the Manchester League, Charlie was beginning to fulfil the promise he had shown in Scottish junior football. He was called up for the Central League side, but played just one reserve match before war broke out. It was a turning point, as he vividly remembered years later, because his reserves debut got off to a nightmare start.

'The first half I couldn't do a thing right. I was worried about doing well, and I came into the dressing-room at half-time crying. Tom Curry put his arm around me and said, "Come on, son, I know you can do it – go out and show them this half." I went out and I played – and that made me. I never again lacked confidence, was never again frightened by an opponent. From then on, Tom Curry was my mentor. I looked to him for advice, correction, for everything. From then on, we'd have this little thing going on between us on match days. I'd always be last to get a rub-down before going out, and he'd come in and say, "Here we go again, son. Let's rub some magic into those legs and then out you go and show them!"'

But turning on the magic for Manchester United in the first team wouldn't happen for five years. Charlie had signed pro forms when he turned 17, and by the time he came to re-sign for the 1939 season, war had been declared. It was then that club secretary Walter Crickmer made Charlie an offer he couldn't refuse.

'Walter said, "Charlie, we're going to sign you on again, and you'll be getting a £20 signing-on fee – £10 now, and another £10 when you come back after the war." That was typical of Walter – always looking after the cash. When I returned to Old Trafford in 1945, the first thing I did was to go and see him. I said, "I'll be happy to sign another contract, Walter, but first you owe me £10." He looked at me and said, "Bloody hell, Charlie, I thought you'd forgotten all about that." And I said, "Do you know, Walter, it's the only thing that's kept me alive.'"

Cheeky Charlie was coming of age. The United starlet had enlisted as a tail-gunner with the RAF and, though he wasn't to know it, bomber aircrews were to suffer one of the highest casualty rates of the war. In the event, a chance meeting with one of soccer's all-time greats on Blackpool promenade changed the course of Charlie Mitten's war.

# 4

# From Buzz-bombs to Busby

We're getting well paid, Charlie – £2 extra for winning! If we weren't here, we'd be getting 10 bob for killing Germans!

Jimmy Bowie, at the 1944 Southern Cup final

FOR CHARLIE MITTEN, THE 1940S STARTED WITH A BANG – and the best-kept little secret of the Second World War. The 1939 season had just got under way when war was declared, and the league programme was frozen, to be resumed with exactly the same fixtures which had been suspended when hostilities started. But the war had also pre-empted a looming clash between the Players Union and the Football League, and this battle was also to be revived in the aftermath of war.

By 1938, gates had begun recovering after the depression years, and the Union was stepping up its campaign for a better deal for players. But within a week of the 1939–40 season starting, the FA had suspended all contracts as the league competition was called off for the duration. The government, however, saw some sort of soccer competition as providing essential, morale-boosting entertainment, so a reorganised fixture list was instituted on the basis of geographical areas which, by the end of the war, had coalesced into North, South and West, most even having their own knockout trophy competitions along the lines of the FA cup. A lot of players joined the war effort, and many were seconded as physical training instructors to promote fitness and morale. These PTIs were encouraged to play in 'internationals' and to turn out for league clubs wherever they were stationed. The stage was set for some memorable clashes on the wartime field of play.

Charlie Mitten was to play his part in many of these matches, but first he was involved in a shoot-out which had nothing to do with penalties, and whose outcome has never before been revealed.

It would not have happened had Charlie been able to tolerate life on the production line at the aircraft factory where he went to work within months of war breaking out. He soon found the indoor work stifling, and it was for this reason that he volunteered for the RAF. He signed on as a radio operator/tail-gunner with Bomber Command and was posted to the south coast for his weapons training.

At a firing range near Brighton, Aircraftsman Mitten proved conclusively that he was somewhat more accurate as a left-wing sharp-shooter than as a rear-gunner. The trainee gunners were paired off in two dozen sandbagged gun emplacements overlooking the sea. A Lysander light aircraft would then be called in, towing some 200 ft behind it a drone plane as target. On the word of the instructor, each of the gunnery crews would let off a burst of ammunition in an attempt to hit the drone as it crossed the line of fire in front of the emplacements. It was the first time Charlie had lined up to shoot anything more deadly than a penalty. This was for real, using live ammo, and what happened next, according to Cheeky Charlie, was still buried deep in the Ministry of Defence archives marked 'Top Secret'.

The way he told it was that on a beautiful clear May day in

1940, the Lysander began its series of target runs on cue, and each of the gun crews up the line duly took it in turns to blast away – some even managing to hit the drone, to cheers all round. Then the Lysander banked for its final run for Charlie's emplacement. The instructor ordered them to pick up the target . . . and . . . *fire*!

There was a burst of machine-gun fire from Charlie's dugout, and 250 yards away over the sea the tail of the Lysander was seen to disintegrate, with the target drone completely unscathed. Seconds later, the stricken Lysander nose-dived into the (fortunately calm) waters of the English Channel. Less than half an hour later, an extremely irate and completely drenched pilot was thundering on to the gunnery range to demand the head of the miserably misbegotten Satan-lover (expletives modified) who had pulled the trigger. To the eternal credit of Charlie's commanding officer, the pilot was given his marching orders, but later the gun crew received the kind of dressing-down you only see in war movies.

Charlie recalled the whole incident with a devilish twinkle in his eye. He insisted it had been his turn to feed the ammo belt to the gun when the Lysander bit the dust – or, more accurately, the waves – and the bullets were going into the firing chamber perfectly straight! He added with a chuckle: 'I didn't think it was a particularly bad shot. It was all hushed up, of course, but I didn't feel this was the kind of shooting for me.'

The War Ministry had little to do with it, but so it turned out: Charlie was posted back up to the north of England to complete his training on a wireless operator's course in Blackpool. The instruction classes were held in the Winter Gardens and, during the lunch-hour break, Charlie would go out for a stroll up the promenade in his uniform. That was when he met Stanley Matthews for the first time.

'He didn't know me, but I knew who he was. By then, he

was a great player and easily recognisable. We were both in RAF uniform – Stan's had sergeant's stripes – and we got chatting. It turned out he was a physical training instructor and organiser of the RAF soccer team. He said, "Why don't you come and see our CO? We need an outside-left." Within a week, Stan had got me switched to a PTI course at Cosford. We got on immediately because we were fellow footballers.'

Thus was Cheeky Charlie's war mapped out. As a qualified PTI and, of course, a top-class footballer in the making, he switched from apprentice to teacher; he was barely 20 years old. By then, he had married a local Manchester girl, Bertha, and was soon to become a family man. These additional responsibilities ensured the early maturing of a confident young man on the field as well as off.

In his last pre-war game for United, a regional match against Blackburn Rovers for whom several Preston stars were guesting, Mitten finally signalled that his talent had arrived. In a 5–2 win, a last-minute goal by Charlie stole the show. As one newspaper put it: 'Nothing transcended the interest of United's fifth goal. Outside-left Mitten secured the ball in his own half and, in a sinuous dribble which took him past man after man, went through on his own to crown a magnificent solo movement with a spectacular goal. This was the thrill of a game of thrills, which never lacked interest right from the start.'

In the 1940–41 season, he guested with Tranmere Rovers and began displaying the prowess that was to fire United after the war. The Merseyside press reported a sensational young star in the making. After Rovers won 5–4 over a Chester side studded with a host of former First Division stars, the *Birkenhead News* concluded: 'Overshadowing everything else was the sparkling Tranmere wing play. The electric raiding and finishing of both Ashcroft and Mitten undoubtedly produced this victory. Stanley Matthews is barely more effective. Mitten is now among the leading goal-scorers.'

Off the pitch, PTI Charlie Mitten was doing well, too. He was soon being entrusted with the setting up of sports facilities and training programmes at RAF airfields. Although far from the front line, the shadow of conflict was ever present: 'I used to pick teams from aircrew lads for matches. Next week, they'd be out of the team – missing, shot down somewhere. It wasn't easy to deal with that sort of thing.'

The man coordinating the PTI programme was Walter Winterbottom, who had played wing-half for United before the war. He had been a schoolteacher before turning professional, and when a serious injury had interrupted his playing career, he turned to the coaching, theory and tactics of the game. During the war, Winterbottom demonstrated his gifts as a brilliant organiser while continuing to turn out as a guest player in League games and being capped as a reserve in two wartime internationals. He, in turn, recognised the capabilities of his former United comrade, appointing Charlie to increasingly important assignments, including a New Forest camp in Hampshire in the build-up to D-Day.

Charlie guested for whatever club was nearest his station. Among his many stops was Southampton, then managed by former Arsenal full-back Tom Parker. Among the squad were Joe Paley, George Tweedie, John Harris and Hearts star Tommy Walker.

The next two seasons Charlie played for Chelsea alongside the likes of Harris and George Hardwick, England's Middlesbrough left-back. They were beaten finalists in the Southern League Cup in 1944 when Charlie found himself up against Allenby Chilton, his future teammate at United, playing for Charlton Athletic. A wartime record crowd of 85,000 – including D-Day commander Dwight Eisenhower – watched the game, and at least 5,000 disappointed fans were left milling around the streets outside Wembley as soccer fever gripped the capital. It's a match Charlie never forgot because it was the only game in his career when he insisted on playing despite being unfit. It was a mistake he never made again.

'I played with a carbuncle on my big toe, and the trainer had to cut the top of my boot out to let the swelling come through. I shouldn't really have turned out, but I had set my heart on playing and Billy Birrell, the Chelsea manager, said, "Well, the decision is yours, Charlie." I must say I felt I let the side down a bit that day.'

Charlie's inside-left that day was Jimmy Bowie, and at centre-forward was Roy Bentley, who went on to play for England. Mitten particularly rated Bowie, perhaps because he saw in him a kindred spirit – irreverent, totally in love with a game they could scarcely believe they were getting paid to play, even with a war on. 'I recall Jimmy saying to me, "We're getting well paid, Charlie – £2 extra for winning! If we weren't here, we'd be getting 10 bob for killing Germans!" We used to get 50 bob, plus expenses, for a game. It doubled our Services wages. The cash went home to my wife, and we kept in touch with the boys.'

It was these wartime contacts which were to prove so invaluable in the building of Manchester United's first post-war team. On the way to that 1944 final, Chelsea knocked out Reading, who had fielded a quietly spoken Scot and polished player at right-half. His name was Matt Busby. The United manager later admitted that he must have subconsciously been thinking ahead as he turned out for these wartime games. Charlie had no doubt: 'Matt realised when he took the job at Old Trafford that he'd seen many of the players who made up the nucleus of that team; people like Chilton, Cockburn, Pearson were already on the club's books when he got there. And, of course, Mitten – although he'd only seen the back of me!'

So did he give Matt Busby a hard time that day? Did Cheeky Charlie 'skin' his future boss? Mitten enigmatically refused to elaborate – save to say, before breaking into a chuckle, that they were not friends on the park that day. (Later, in 1999, Charlie told his nephew Andy, writing for *United We Stand* magazine: "Matt was a good player, but he wasn't quick enough [to catch] me, and I gave him a hard time.")

Another vivid, more serious memory was of a game at Stamford Bridge after the threat from the Luftwaffe had faded. London matches by then were attracting crowds at pre-war levels. But even Cheeky Charlie was dumbstruck by one of the first pilot-less, so-called 'Doodlebug' flying-bomb attacks.

'There must have been 30,000 people inside the ground that day when, in the middle of the match, the whole ground went into a deathly hush. There we were, still playing, and you couldn't hear a whisper from the terraces – it was bloody eerie. We were wondering what we'd done wrong, when we heard that faint BRRRRRR overhead. We looked up and saw this buzz-bomb going across the rooftops, just over from the stadium. Then it cut out, crashed and exploded. You could hear the dull ZZZZ! WHUMP! shake the stadium. Then, suddenly, everyone went back to normal, and were shouting and cheering because it hadn't dropped on the ground.'

Charlie recalled that his next posting came as a similar bombshell. Walter Winterbottom assigned him to the Azores for the final year of the war. Charlie felt he'd been doing a good job and asked himself what he'd done to deserve this posting. He'd settled in at the Hampshire aerodrome in the New Forest, where the HQ was a magnificent country mansion and his wife and two children were living nearby in a bungalow. Charlie was even keeping chickens for a steady supply of eggs. He admitted he hadn't a clue what the Azores were, never mind where they were, and he feared the worst.

The posting meant that his family had to return to Manchester and live at his parents' home in Skirton Road, Old Trafford. Charlie's family had moved down to Manchester from Scotland six months after he joined United to be near him. His father went to work at Metro-Vickers in Trafford Park, but was away in the Army training corps in the Hebrides during the war.

The Azores station was an RAF Coastal Command refuelling base for the long-range aircraft which patrolled the Atlantic and provided submarine-hunter cover for the convoys, as well as a halfway stopover for flights to and from the United States. Indeed, there were a lot of American servicemen stationed on the islands and they were able to turn out a useful soccer side.

Charlie ended up thanking rather than cursing Walter Winterbottom for his final posting. The Azores didn't turn out to be as bad as he'd feared – although, as he recalled, soccer pitches had to be literally carved out of the volcanic soil of the islands with bulldozers. But inter-Services matches and fixtures against local Portuguese sides proved a great success as well as being stiff competition, drawing crowds of 30,000 and more. In their close-control ball skills, he had an inkling of what was to come. Almost inevitably, Charlie, by now a veteran soccer organiser, fielded a British Forces XI which remained unbeaten to the end of the war. The team included Liverpool's Ray Lambert and Stan Matthews' elder brother Ron at centre-half. In between, he played in inter-unit matches – in one, achieving a prodigious record by scoring all 13 goals from the centre-forward position in a 13–2 victory. It's a feat unbeaten in the Azores – and possibly anywhere in the world – to this day.

With so many Yanks on station, Charlie also got to meet two up-and-coming American 'youngsters' in another branch of showbusiness – troop entertainment party guys, Frank Sinatra and Phil Silvers, who subsequently became firm favourites of Charlie's. And he made a very important soccer contact, which turned into a lifelong friendship. Antonio Borges Coutinho owned the pineapple-growing island of San

Miguel and later (1969–76) became president of Benfica. When Charlie's playing days were over, the crack Portuguese side would be among the host of world-class teams which he took on match tours all over the world in his capacity as a UEFA promoter.

The war robbed Charlie, along with many other players, of six of the most productive years of his career. After his demob in the Azores, he returned to Manchester with a kitbag full of pineapples from the future Benfica president and a burning desire to make his mark and his fortune in the game that was his whole life. But like all the other players coming back from the war, he was returning to a Football League set-up light years out of step with the new spirit of the times, as a Labour landslide swept wartime leader Winston Churchill out of power and a new government took over, promising a new age for the working man.

All players had to return to their parent clubs, even though all contracts had been expired for five years. That was the rule. The hierarchy believed that once you'd signed for a club, irrespective of the terms or length of the contract, you were theirs for life. Professional footballers were serfs in everything but name.

# 5

# Reds Star Rising

Bloody hell, Charlie, this [United] team you've got here
could win the ... Boat Race!

Bill Shankly, 1947

THE RAIN WAS POURING THROUGH THE ROOF, THE STANDS
were blitzed hulks and the pitch an unplayable crust of cinders
when the players began reporting back to Old Trafford in
1945. The ground had paid dearly for its proximity to the
tempting industrial target of Trafford Park during the war. If
that wasn't bad enough, what none of the players, including
Charlie Mitten, could know was that Manchester United was
also virtually bankrupt, living day to day on a £15,000
overdraft. Charlie's most abiding memory of his first few
weeks back training at United was of the gaggle of dishevelled
figures, old sweaters and slacks worn over shirts and jerseys,
jogging around the ground looking for all the world like a
bunch of tramps on the run. Things didn't look promising,
and the group of players who had joined Old Trafford as
youngsters before the war were now mature young footballing
lions who had no idea what they were capable of. But there
was one man at the club who did.

He was Matt Busby, the club's new manager. The former Scotland international had been at Liverpool just before the war after years of sterling service with United's local rivals, Manchester City. But he had no previous connection with United, and the players hadn't a clue how he'd come to take over, nor could they imagine the kind of transformation he was soon to bring about.

'The club was really down in the dumps; the main stand had been blitzed and the pitch was unfit to play on. We were told we'd have to play all our home games at Manchester City's ground – which we did for three years. In those immediate post-war days, we were readjusting ourselves to League football and getting to know a new manager in very difficult conditions. But our impression of Matt from the first was that this was a club that was going to achieve great things. From the very start, we found him sincere and straight from the shoulder, and we soon realised that in Matt Busby we had a leader of outstanding ability.'

Busby had, in fact, taken over as the result of a secret approach by Louis Rocca, United's chief scout, who had tried to sign him from Manchester City when he was a player there 15 years before. The Lanarkshire man had joined the Maine Road club in 1928 at the age of 18, though he'd initially failed to make an impact as an inside-forward and had had to struggle for a regular first-team place. In 1931, City were prepared to transfer him, but United couldn't afford the nominal fee of £150. 'We couldn't even afford 150 shillings,' Rocca recalled. In fact, Christmas 1930 had been the absolute nadir of United's fortunes. The National Provincial Bank in Spring Gardens, Manchester, had withdrawn credit facilities and the club had been unable even to guarantee players' summer wages.

The man who came to the rescue was James Gibson, a successful Manchester textile manufacturer who stepped in with a £40,000 guarantee to the bank. The Gibson family papers reveal that the club was only able to maintain the tradition of a free turkey for all staff at Christmas 1930 because Gibson insisted on paying for them out of his own pocket. When Gibson in effect assumed full control of the club in January 1931, the accounts revealed that there was just £100 in the trust fund for new players. That included a postal order for one shilling from a fan who said he couldn't make it to Old Trafford on Saturdays, but who hoped his contribution would help keep the club going, nevertheless.

Busby stayed at City for the time being, switching to wing-half – and was transformed. He became the midfield creative force which inspired City to two FA Cup finals. In 1934, after City beat Portsmouth 2–1, Busby was described as the finest right-half ever seen at Wembley. That same afternoon, United were drawing 1–1 with Swansea to avoid relegation from the Second Division.

Throughout most of the 1930s, United had languished in the Second Division. After gaining promotion in 1936, they slipped back the following season, only to return to the First behind Aston Villa, exchanging places for the first time with Manchester City, who had by then transferred Busby to Liverpool.

Now, in 1945, Rocca saw another opportunity to bring Busby to Old Trafford, this time as manager. He wrote a confidential letter to Company Sergeant-Major Busby, then stationed as a PTI in Italy. A meeting between Busby and club chairman James Gibson was arranged, and on 15 February 1945, at a Trafford Park canalside cold-storage building two miles from United's bombed-out ground, Busby made his all or nothing demand: full control of the team and five years to do the job. 'I had no experience as a manager. All I had was ideas and faith in the future of the club,' he later recalled. Gibson thanked Busby for his 'honesty of purpose', and the deal was done.

What a derelict club now had was a completely new kind of

manager, a man confident in his own knowledge of the game after a distinguished playing career, one who was young enough to train in a tracksuit with his players – and a man with a vision. His experience at Manchester City and Liverpool had convinced him that to get the best from his players he had to work closely with them to understand their individual psychology and to gain their respect. But Busby also had luck on his side.

He was fortunate to have come to a club which, though in the worst possible physical and financial circumstances, had a priceless advantage few other clubs in the League had: at least seven home-grown senior players who were immediately of world-class potential. They included Johnny Carey, who was in Italy; Pearson and Morris, who were both in India; Chilton, who was guesting with Reading and, of course, Mitten, who was still in the Azores. When Charlie finally came home in 1946 and made his League debut for United, he was 25 years old. As Busby said at the time: 'The future looks fine. United have a first-class side if I could only get them together in one place.'

Busby's only key signing was Jimmy Delaney, transferred from Celtic for £4,000. Though already 31, the balding winger, whose injury-prone record earned him the nickname 'Brittle Bones', completed the attacking line-up that was to win the FA Cup in 1948. (Delaney went on to achieve a unique treble when he won a Northern Ireland FA Cup-winners medal in 1954, having already earned a Scottish Cup-winners medal with Celtic in 1937.)

Charlie recalled those early line-ups: Crompton, Griffiths, Roughton, Warner, Chilton, Cockburn, Delaney, Morris, Rowley, Pearson and Mitten. Billy Wrigglesworth had been playing outside-left, but Mitten displaced him when he was demobbed. Two seasons later, United's Wembley side for the FA Cup final against Blackpool consisted of Crompton, Carey, Aston, Anderson, Chilton, Cockburn, Delaney, Morris,

Rowley, Pearson and Mitten. 'You can see that Matt took over a very good side after the war. But to Matt goes the credit for moulding us into a great team.'

In fact, it was widely believed that Gibson had paid for Delaney out of his own pocket. In the early months, there were several tense altercations on transfer policy between Busby and his chairman. On one occasion, Gibson waved a stick at Busby and ordered him to go out and 'buy or else'. Ten years earlier, Gibson's autocratic style had led to the resignation of Scott Duncan over precisely the same issue.

It happened after Gibson had signed 19-year-old Jack Rowley for £3,000 from Bournemouth while on holiday – and without informing Duncan, making the manager's position untenable. Duncan, a Scotland international who had played for Rangers and Newcastle United, had told the *Manchester Evening News* on his arrival at the club that he wouldn't buy stars; he would 'make them, rather than buy them. I would rather build soundly and well, creating a good all-round average than have an unbalanced side with two of the greatest football stars in the country.' He believed in finding talented youngsters – like Charlie Mitten, whom he had signed in 1936 – and bringing them on.

The question of the precise balance between home-grown and imports was clearly at issue, and Duncan's authority was being undermined. In the event, pressures from the board and the supporters for instant success led to mixed fortunes. In the 1934 season alone, no fewer than 38 players were used in the first team as new men were bought and sold in the search for a successful formula. In 1935–36, United won promotion to the First Division only to be relegated the following year, and Duncan ended up parting company with the club over his diminishing control.

But, in 1947, Gibson met his match. Busby was resolute; he knew he already had the players – he'd seen most of them in action and had even played with some of them – and rather than be bounced into spending more of the chairman's personal cash on transfers, he wanted first to exploit the assets he believed the club already had. Gibson later apologised and Busby gained complete control over team policy. He had won a crucial political battle.

What impressed the players about Busby's management style was his genuine concern for their welfare. At a time when housing was extremely difficult to find, all married players were offered a modern semi-detached house to rent from the club. Everyone was treated the same, and no one ever had to ask for any of his financial entitlements such as bonuses or allowances. It brought a rare spirit of trust between club and players at a time when the League and the Players Union had once again locked horns in the dispute shelved in 1939, and which threatened to spill over into a strike in the first months after the end of the war. By prevarication and bluster, the League bought off the threat by raising the £8 pre-war maximum to £9.

At Old Trafford, though the club was bound by the League's formula, the attitude towards players tempered the feudal relationship between club and players, as Charlie fondly recalled: 'It soon became evident to all on the United payroll that the new manager took a very personal interest in each one of us and in our playing careers. I am always thankful to this day that Matt Busby took the trouble to analyse my strengths and weaknesses. He did it with all of us, but he never just criticised and then left you without the answer. Matt knew the remedy to the hundred and one things that can go wrong with a professional footballer's game. Matt encouraged us, too, to analyse each other's faults at straight-talking sessions – with no punches pulled. We found this honesty made us a much more formidable team.'

Maybe it worked because of Matt Busby's sense of decency and fair play – a contrast perhaps to the ordering about they'd had to put up with in the Services. 'It was the secret of the wonderful team spirit in the side. I thought it was the greatest team I'd ever played for in my life. It was very much a case of the cog-wheels in a good machine clicking – although like any other team, of course, we had an occasional off-day.'

In fact, they had very few. Matt Busby realised that he had the players to experiment with a more fluid, attacking style of football. In October 1945, 11 factory-team players, each carrying a gift of a bouquet of flowers out onto the pitch for the opposing team before kick-off, had arrived in Britain for a short exhibition tour. They were Dynamo Moscow, and the press dismissed them as slow amateurs. But they played a flowing, relentlessly attacking game that was a revelation. They drew 3–3 with Chelsea and 2–2 with Rangers, won 4–3 against the mighty Arsenal (for whom Matthews and Mortensen were guesting) and demolished Cardiff 10–1. Charlie recalled their effect on Busby: 'Matt saw them play and was impressed. He thought this all-out-attack style was perfectly suited to the kind of players he'd inherited at Old Trafford. He was fortunate in that he started out with a very good side. This gave him three or four seasons to allow his managerial talents to develop.'

In this sense, Busby was very much reliant on the cohesiveness of his players. In 1947, United finished runners-up to Busby's pre-war team, Liverpool, and the following season were again second, this time to Arsenal, who drew a record 83,260 crowd for their away game against United at Maine Road. The team made a bad start, losing their early games, as Johnny Morris recalled: 'We were struggling – I think we'd only managed to get one point – so Matt called a special meeting with the players one Friday. He called us into the dressing-room instead of training and said, "We can't go on like this; we've got to sort it out. What are we going to do about it?" So Allen Chilton says to Matt, "You sit in the corner and be quiet, and *we'll* sort it out." In the team talk, Chilly got on to one or two players – I won't mention names – but he told them, "If I was picking the team, I'd leave you in t' bath!" Allen was like that. Next day we were playing at Preston, who were top of the league, and we beat them 6–1. That's when we knew we had a good side. Of course, Matt got all the credit.'

At Deepdale, the formidable Preston North End line-up included the elusive versatility of Tom Finney and the wing-half steel of Bill Shankly. The great Shanks, understandably, felt that a comfortable win was not an impossibility against a side that seemed to be going nowhere. As they were coming off the pitch, Charlie recalled a rueful Shankly telling him: 'Bloody hell, Charlie, this team you've got here could win the f*****g Boat Race!'

By the end of the 1947–48 season, perhaps Charlie & Co. could indeed have given Oxbridge a run for their money – on the Irwell, of course! Certainly, it was United's winning the 1948 FA Cup – generally regarded as the best final ever – that finally signalled that a new force had arrived in English football. United had reached the final having played First Division opposition in every round, including Aston Villa in an epic, heart-stopping contest which still rates as one of the greatest-ever cup-ties. Racing into a 5–1 lead, United had finally won 6–4 in a feast of goal thrills. It was a tie full of vivid incident and characters, as Charlie recalled: 'When you come into the dressing-room at the interval with a 5–1 lead, you're bound to think the game is all over bar the shouting. But Villa, always a good footballing side, really set about us in the second half. I'll always remember the ref in charge, a tremendously fit man, who was running faster than some of the players, and always well up with play. He was right there when I chipped a ball to Stan Pearson, who put his arms out preparing to chest it down. But in the tension of the game, the ref anticipated too quickly, thinking that Stan was going to handle it, and blew his whistle for a foul. In fact, the next split second, Pearson merely chested the ball in a perfectly legal manner. Disgusted with the wrong decision, I turned angrily to the ref, shouting, "Mr Evans, Mr Evans . . ." Smilingly, the ref interrupted my tirade: "I know, Charles. I know you're going to tell me what to do with my whistle!"

'Another stunning incident was when Villa got a free-kick about 20 yards out and Dickie Dorsett stepped up to take it. We lined up to block the kick, and I was the end man in the wall as usual, marking their winger. Dickie was well known for his cannon-ball shot, and I'll always remember Allenby Chilton, Henry Cockburn, Johnny Carey and all the boys lining up as Dorsett took a tremendous run-up and hit one of his cannon balls – straight into the net. There was only Chilton left standing – everybody else "melted". If that shot of Dickie's had hit one of our lads, it would have bored a hole clean through him!'

United went on to win every tie by at least two goals without one replay, often having to play their home ties as far afield as Huddersfield and Goodison Park when Maine Road was needed for City's own commitments. Mitten scored in victories against Liverpool (3–0), Charlton (2–0) and Preston (4–1). The semi-final against Charlton Athletic at Huddersfield was another game he particularly remembered, because of a superb show by Charlton's long-serving goalkeeper Sam Bartram, who later went on to manage York City. 'We peppered the Charlton goal, as Bartram made some absolutely incredible saves. His goal-kicks got shorter and shorter as the game wore on because Big Sam was so exhausted with the amount of work we'd given him. Sam Bartram was one of the greatest goalkeepers never capped for England. A great player and first-class club-man.'

Having got through the semis, the six-week wait till the final was a nervous time for the players – to say nothing of the manager. 'Players are frightened to go all out in the tackle in the weeks before – and that's the time when injuries are, paradoxically, more likely,' said Charlie. 'When you are taking half-chances, jumping to get out of the way, then you're more likely to get injured. Matt Busby's advice to us during those nervous weeks was: play your normal game, and it will keep you out of trouble.'

The final was a game Charlie Mitten never forgot. United arrived at Wembley aware that this was their moment of truth. Busby's reputation as a manager had been based on his simple philosophy that his players should go out and enjoy their game first, rather than concern themselves with elaborate questions of tactics. As Charlie recalled: 'Matt was always quietly persuasive. We had very few team talks about tactics. He'd just say, "Boys, you're all good players, go out and express yourselves and, most importantly, enjoy the game." He believed that football was a simple game that didn't need complicated tactical plans to be played well.'

But on the occasion of their first major trophy, Busby faltered. United, still very much the up-and-coming team, were playing against a resurgent Blackpool side that included the two Stans – Matthews, who had moved from Stoke the previous season in a controversial £11,000 transfer, and Mortensen, a fearsome goal machine who had replaced Raich 'The Wraith' Carter in the England line-up.

Busby was acutely conscious of Matthews' reputation – that season, the Wizard of Dribble had single-handedly destroyed Belgium and Northern Ireland in internationals – and Matt decided on containment tactics on United's left side in a bid to smother the right-wing threat. This meant pulling Charlie back from his normal all-out attacking role.

'The tactics were to try and keep Stan quiet. Johnny Aston would jockey him, and I was to come from the back and harass him and take the ball off him. Well, I chased Stan up and down the line, and I thought, "I'm getting out of breath here for nothing." When you chased Stan, you'd got to move a bit. I was sharp, but I couldn't seem to get near him, and nothing was happening. As we were walking off at half-time, Stan turns to me and says, "You know, Charlie, you'll never be a good player if you keep chasing me. Buzz off into your own half!" "Chasing you?" I said. "I can't get bloody near you!"'

As United's forward line spluttered, Blackpool came off at the interval 2–1 up. Charlie recalled the half-time council of war in the United dressing-room: 'We said, "Boss, this is not the way we generally play; we always attack!" So Matt says, "OK, boys, off you go! But keep playing the football – and it's bound to come out right." We came out, scored three goals and won. Busby always knew when to change tactics. In the first half, we were more negative, trying to neutralise *their* strengths. But all the players felt ill at ease playing that way. We weren't clicking at all. In the second half, we went back to our normal game. It turned out to be one of the laziest games I ever played in my life.'

The *News of the World* praised the United forward line: 'The second half was definitely United's. Some of the attacking moves of Delaney, Morris, Rowley, Pearson and Mitten were brilliant in the extreme.' No wonder United eventually ran out winners 4–2 in a game now acknowledged to have been a classic – even better than the Matthews final of 1953, which was very much a one-man show. The 1948 final was marked by electrifying attacking play from both sides, particularly from predatory goal-takers whom we now call strikers. (United's right-half Johnny Anderson ruefully reflected that his 35-yard screamer which finally buried Blackpool was the only goal the Pathé newsreel team missed.) For Blackpool, there was Mortensen, known as the Electric Eel because of his ability to wriggle through massed defences. He was a goalmouth moocher supreme, later matched only by Jimmy Greaves and perhaps Gary Lineker. And, of course, there were United's Stan Pearson of the silky body swerve, Jack Rowley, who had dynamite in his boots and could head the ball harder than some players can kick it, and the mercurial Johnny Morris. Charlie believed their kind of flair was sorely missed in the modern game.

'They had one thing in mind when they got the ball anywhere near goal – and they didn't mess around looking for people to pass it to. They'd go for it, and they didn't often miss. If you were looking for someone to pull a match out of the fire, they were the ones who could do it. Today, how many times do you see a team not able to attack the goal like this? They get the ball to the edge of the box and they can't seem to attack the goal – and that's down to no confidence due to a lack of ball skills. That's what we should be concentrating on today.'

The FA Cup final, Charlie believed, was the one big occasion that tested even the most experienced and self-possessed player. Anyone who claims he is not affected by 'Wembley nerves' before the game is either kidding himself or is not normal. It's the one match every footballer wants to play in and the one he most fears losing. Charlie remembered United's burly centre-half Allenby Chilton standing in the dressing-room ready to go out before the 1948 final with all his football kit on but still wearing his shoes, due to the pressures of the occasion.

'I've been asked many times what was the most memorable day in my football career, and it was without doubt to play at Wembley in the FA Cup final. This is unquestionably the greatest day in a professional footballer's life. Even though we arrived at Wembley after scoring twenty-two goals in six ties, there were few of us who weren't jumpy. I remember right up to the kick-off I was warming my feet in hot water to get the circulation going.'

But does the pressure explain why there have been so few exciting Cup finals? Why has the standard of play so rarely matched up to the great occasion? A glance at the record over the last ten years makes for depressing reading: 1996, Manchester United 1, Liverpool 0; 1997, Chelsea 2, Middlesbrough 0; 1998, Arsenal 2, Newcastle 0; 1999, Manchester United 2, Newcastle 0; 2000, Chelsea 1, Aston

Villa 0; 2001, Liverpool 2, Arsenal 1; 2002, Arsenal 2, Chelsea 0; 2003, Arsenal 1, Southampton 0; 2004, Manchester United 3, Millwall 0; 2005, Arsenal 0, Manchester United 0 – with Arsenal winning 5–4 on penalties.

Charlie believed it was because in most finals the teams, usually of the same strength and ability, come to give nothing away. As a result, the FA's showpiece match often ends up a 'spoiling game', with both sides afraid of losing and unwilling to play. Which was conspicuously not the case in 1948.

'It was certainly sheer football that pulled us back from behind to take the coveted FA Cup back to Old Trafford. It was a crowning glory on a memorable season. The game in that Cup-run which stands out in my mind was the first-round clash with Aston Villa. What a battle! We won 6–4, but before the game the bookies were offering 28–1 against us winning the Cup. But even at that stage, we fancied ourselves to win. We heard one or two prominent Manchester businessmen had a wager on us, one getting back £28,000!'

Manchester United had arrived. Mitten believed that United's first post-war side was the equal if not better than any since, including that team of flowering talents which was so tragically cut down in the Munich air crash.

'I think that if there had been a European Cup at this time, we would certainly have been winners. Individually, of course, the United side which was so tragically decimated at Munich had some great players but, by and large, I think we had a much harder striking force. Every player in our side had an individual quality about him that was the hallmark of a great side indeed. There was nothing we wouldn't do for each other off the field and on the pitch. Each player had supreme confidence in every one of his colleagues.'

And so, of course, did Matt. And if in 1950 United faltered, slipping to finish fourth, albeit only three points behind champions Portsmouth, one man, at least, in the red shirt of Manchester United remained razor sharp at the ultimate skill which today is defeating even the best players in the world. It's a skill in which Matt Busby himself had been tested and found wanting. A sudden-death skill which too many modern-day commentators attribute to fickle fortune. And it's called on during those three seconds that can make or break even the masters of the world.

# 6

# The Penalty King

The story is told of the Master who, after many years,
agreed to demonstrate his artless art. From 60 feet, the
flame of a candle placed before a target was extinguished.
The student lit a torch and, in the flickering light, saw that
two arrows had been fired, the second splitting the first
from the knock, right down the shaft. Master, how did you
do this? cried his pupil. And the Master replied, I did not
do it – IT does it!

Adapted from *Zen in the Art of Archery* by Eugen Herrigel

THAT ONE MOMENT WHICH EVERY PLAYER DREADS, THAT SLIM
window of opportunity for fame and glory in three seconds
which seem like an eternity, came to Eddie Souza at Fall River
Stadium, Massachusetts, in June 1950. Souza was the talented
inside-left of the New England All-Stars who were playing the
visiting team from the home of soccer. It was Manchester
United's third game of a nationwide tour and would prove to
be the hardest. The All-Stars turned out several players who
later that summer were part of the United States World Cup
squad in South America.

Like the rest of the 12-match tour, this was an exhibition

game – but it was no stroll. The New Englanders were determined to halt the Limey invaders who had already won their two opening games against a backdrop of fevered interest in soccer due to the upcoming World Cup finals.

United had taken the lead after only ten minutes when outside-right Tom Bogan pounced to keep the ball in play when it looked to be going over for a goal-kick on the right wing. With the All-Stars defence caught square, the American keeper, Walt Romanowicz, rushed off his line to close down the winger. But Bogan coolly clipped the ball to the incoming Jack Rowley who blasted in an unstoppable low volley. Instead of caving in, the All-Stars, inspired by some acrobatic saves from Romanowicz, counter-attacked. With 12 minutes remaining, Allenby Chilton conceded a penalty and Eddie Souza stepped up. He hit it well, beating United's Jack Crompton, but the ball cannoned back off the post. The chance had gone. United raced away to score a flattering goal two minutes from time.

The New England press reported a 'lively' battle studded with individual flashes of brilliance – especially from Charlie Mitten. 'The Manchester outside [*sic*] player thrilled with a masterful display of ball control and dribbling,' noted one paper. The *Manchester Evening News* special correspondent reported that Mitten had been the 'outstanding player on the field' in a 'rugged' match. But would Cheeky Charlie, United's deputed spot-kick taker, have done better than Souza in such a charged atmosphere had the Manchester team been awarded a penalty?

Honours might have been shared had Eddie Souza seized his moment of glory. But he has been in the best of company, as when Roberto Baggio blasted over in a sudden-death shoot-out to lose Italy the World Cup in 1994. There have been few players anywhere in the world who could claim never to have failed at football's ultimate solo challenge.

And the technique of the world's top-flight players has

consistently proved woefully inadequate season after season since. The 2005-06 campaign has so far been no different – at home and abroad. As recently as October, Real Madrid's iconic playmaker Zinedine Zidane cost the Galacticos valuable points when he shot wide in a game against Valencia, who until the penalty award had been struggling against an attack led by the twinkled-toed Robinho. But the moment passed, and Real paid the price going down to a Valencia penalty three minutes from time. But Zidane was in good company that weekend. At the Reebok stadium, Dio Kamara blazed over after his first successful penalty had to be re-taken. And at Higbury there was a moment of high farce that's sure to be immortalised by the Trivial Pursuit question gauleiters – a penalty-spot trick by Robert Pires misfired, and his miscued side-pass left a waiting Thierry Henry mouthing a bit more than 'Va-Va Voom!' Manager Arsène Wenger's sanguine interpretation of his players' attempt to emulate Johann Cruyff's trick penalty against Barcelona in 1982 was that Pires had been 'a bit insecure about taking a second penalty'. Pires's successful spot-kick 11 minutes earlier proved to be the difference between an unlucky Manchester City and Arsenal. The reaction of Manchester City boss Stuart Pearce was, as ever, generous and Delphic. But, then, he has a lot to be philosophical about.

The former England star, with the most intimidating nickname in the game, twice had occasion to recall his own *annus horribilis* – 1990 – when he (and Chris Waddle) failed in the World Cup penalty shoot-out against the Germans. In May 2005, his team lost out in the UEFA Cup against Middlesbrough after City's £10 million yesterday man Robbie Fowler failed to beat Mark Schwarzer from the spot two minutes into added time. Then, within weeks of the start of the new season, the Sky Blue millionaires were blown out of the Carling Cup by Doncaster Rovers 3–0 in the sudden death shoot-out that followed a 1–1 extra-time draw.

And so it goes on with, it seems, nothing likely to change any time soon. In the season I interviewed Charlie Mitten for this book, 1996, the FA Cup-final line-up was determined by spot-kicks, as round after round was settled by penalty shoot-outs that separated the men from the masters. Teddy Sheringham blew it for Spurs in the fifth-round replay against Nottingham Forest; in the third round, Chelsea put out Newcastle in a sudden-death shoot-out which followed their replay at Stamford Bridge. Among those off target at the Bridge was Peter Beardsley. It happened again in the next round – this time Queens Park Rangers going out to Chelsea, after Bradley Allen had missed the chance of equalising with only minutes remaining. Queens Park Rangers manager and former England and United star Ray Wilkins was solicitous about his striker Bradley Allen's miss that put out Rangers. 'The best players in the world miss penalties – look at the World Cup,' averred Butch in the TV post-mortem.

On the same programme, former England star Gary Lineker was equally full of commiserations: it could happen to anyone. This is especially so now that so many games are on TV, so everyone can see the way you take a spot-kick – which side of the goal you aim for. 'With penalties, you know that from time to time you're going to miss,' quoth the poacher turned crisp front man.

Matt Busby would also have sympathised. He knew the feeling well: you wish the ground would open up and swallow you. During the last weeks of the war, in April 1945, he had been captain when Scotland took on England at Hampden Park, and the Scots were awarded a penalty with the auld enemy ahead at 3–1. A goal then might have transformed the game. As it was, the England goalkeeper, Frank Swift, saved, and Busby's side was routed 6–1. What made the defeat especially bitter for the future United manager was that *he* was the penalty-taker who missed. It later transpired that Busby had asked two of his teammates to take the spot-kick; both had refused. Neither dared accept the responsibility. But the whole episode is even more curious. Swift was the Manchester City goalkeeper and Busby had befriended him when Swift first joined the Maine Road club as a youth player. Busby had regularly helped Swift practise dealing with spot-kicks. A case of the pupil outwitting the teacher? Maybe.

But Cheeky Charlie Mitten said his boss had no excuse. No one, but no one, should ever fail to score a penalty. Not even himself. And yet that's precisely what he did in the very next game after that charged day at Massachusetts – and Charlie never forgave himself.

It was a spot-kick blank with the whole world watching, and it made the post-match headlines. It happened at the Randall's Island stadium in New York against an American League All-Star XI in what was described as one of the greatest soccer games ever seen in the Land of the Free. United were trailing 2–1, and Charlie had been marked out of the game by a resolute Yankee defence determined not to give the Reds' left-wing imp an inch. As the *Manchester Evening News* special correspondent reported with a degree of understatement: 'Mitten was well watched and not allowed much headway.'

Charlie's shot was superbly saved by goalkeeper Duncan McPhail, whose performance throughout the game had been sublime, and it was only a late header by Johnny Aston, drafted into the forward line, that saved the day. Charlie recalled: 'It was one of the toughest games I ever played in – and my concentration went. But there was no excuse for the miss; there never is with a penalty.'

Mitten was the penalty specialist supreme. According to the *Daily Express*, he never missed, and Charlie would always chuckle when he made the distinction between shooting wide and having a spot-kick saved. He was adamant he never missed the target, and admitted to only two brilliantly saved kicks – one on a rock-hard icy pitch in a January cup-tie. (The statistics say it *could* be four.) In his four glorious seasons with

Manchester United, Mitten scored 18 goals from the penalty spot – a record that stood for more than 50 years. On the way to amassing that total, he equalled another record which had stood for almost 30 years – three penalties in one game. It was a feat first achieved by Billy Walker of Aston Villa in a First Division game against Bradford City in November 1921. Charlie matched it in 1950, but it was the manner in which he did so that has gone down in the annals of footballing legend.

By an uncanny coincidence, Aston Villa again figured in the game. It was United's first season back at Old Trafford, and the man facing Charlie was Villa's experienced Joe Rutherford, who had an intimidating reputation as a penalty-saver. In the 1946–47 season, he'd memorably saved two spot-kicks in the same match, against Everton at Goodison Park. So the Old Trafford eyeball-to-eyeball confrontation had all the overtones of a classic Hollywood Western shoot-out.

Come the first penalty, and Mitten steps up, places the ball on the spot and steps back four paces, never taking his eyes off the Villa goalkeeper – and whack! The ball hits the left-hand corner stanchion high up and bounces out. Then comes number two. Cheeky Charlie goes through exactly the same routine. Whack! Again the left-hand stanchion is rattled. Then came that super-charged moment when United were awarded their third penalty. We have the personal testimony of on-pitch eyewitnesses Henry Cockburn, Stan Pearson and Allenby Chilton to thank for the following account of what happened next. A palpable hush descends on an expectant crowd. The atmosphere is electric. Will it be Mitten again? Has anyone scored three penalties in one game? Surely it's too much to expect him to put away a third?

No, it wasn't too much. Busby knew it, and so did Charlie Mitten. There was no hesitation from Manchester United's diminutive penalty king as he stepped forward to take his third spot-kick. It was the same deliberate ritual, like a robot on auto-pilot. But before Charlie could step back, Joe Rutherford stepped forward a couple of paces. Allenby Chilton, who said he regarded Mitten as the best penalty-taker he'd ever seen, remembered the Villa keeper's exact words: 'Where's this one going, Charlie?' Both he and Stan Pearson recalled their utter disbelief at the reply: 'Same place.' The keeper's attempt to unsettle him was a nice try. But penalty goal number three it was – and in exactly the same place. Charlie ended up with four goals in that game – the other a rare header – in a match that ended 7–0, with United playing some of their best ever soccer.

An Old Trafford favourite of the 1990s who came close to overhauling Charlie's record with Gallic style was the mercurial Eric Cantona. His ice-cool double penalty strike in the 1994 FA Cup final against Chelsea ensured a famous League and Cup Double for the Reds. But the lure of the big screen intervened, and United's French lieutenant departed to seek another kind of fame. If the high-kicking Cantona had made it to his total, Charlie would have been the first to congratulate him. Charlie always believed the beautiful game is bigger than its biggest stars; what's important is how it's played. Mitten was ever gracious to those who turned it on, week after week, on the park – even after he had long given up involvement in football.

It's no wonder he has the utmost respect for those who can deliver when the chips are down in the most challenging three seconds ever to face a player. For it will be a sure sign that they are serious and have worked at it. Charlie did. His cheekiness was born of utter confidence. Speak to anyone who ever played with him and they'll tell you the same. 'He was the best penalty-taker in the country,' averred post-war centre-half rock Chilton. Charlie even claimed he bet Sam Bartram, whom he knew well, that he wouldn't save the penalty – even after telling him which side it was going. Indeed, according to Henry Cockburn, United's cultured left-half in that first post-war side, the opposing goalkeeper never had any doubt where

Charlie's penalties were going. 'Charlie *always* told the keeper where he was going to put it – and he never missed. That's why he got called Cheeky Charlie.'

Henry was a product of United's first youth policy, joining the club as a teenager from his home town of Ashton-under-Lyne. Cockburn, who was only 5 ft 4 in. but could outjump players who towered over him, went on to win 13 caps for England. He told me before his death in 2003: 'Charlie was not only a very good player with a lovely left foot, but a great bloke who was so easy to get on with. I missed him when he went to Fulham, and I was always surprised he never played for England again.'

That 'lovely left foot' was in fact the secret of Charlie Mitten's success. Commentators ceaselessly marvelled at its precision. Once, after watching Mitten at Craven Cottage, the legendary radio commentator John Arlott wrote: 'It is in parting with the ball that Mitten is at his finest. His left foot is a precision instrument as accurate as any in contemporary football. You see it in his equally perfect placing of the fast, short ball, and of the 40-yard drive from a retreat position which penetrates a defence direct to the foot of a colleague in front of goal. The accuracy of his centring is such that he can pick his man, adjust his length to the near post, the far post or the opposite winger. Then there is the left-foot shot which makes him among the most dangerous marksmen among our wingers, a shot executed with a swing as polished and as perfectly tuned as a cover drive by Hutton.'

Teammate Johnny Morris put it a shade more colourfully: 'If he could hit a golf ball as straight as he could kick a football, he'd have been a top-ranking Ryder Cup star. I could pass the ball from the inside-right position to him on the wing, run forward at the far post, and it would be on the end of my toe in the box. It was never a chance cross – he'd place them every time. Stan Matthews used to place them too, but Charlie placed them travelling twice as fast. They were very difficult for defenders to get at, and we used to score goals off them all the time. He was a natural. Charlie could do anything with a dead ball, he was so accurate. I can never remember him missing a penalty at United. He was full of tricks on the wing: he used to trap the ball with his backside – brilliant! He could beat a man; he had the speed, and he was so quick-thinking. And he never missed one if you put it on his left foot in the box. He was also one of the nicest lads you could meet.'

It was these unequalled skills that later earned Charlie a place in Matt Busby's all-time greatest 'dream team'. 'Cheeky Charlie made it look like a precision job when he crossed the ball. And when he cut in and let fly with his left, his aim was deadly,' wrote Busby.

In Busby's best-ever team, Mitten was in the cultured company of Alex Stepney, Johnny Carey, Allenby Chilton, Duncan Edwards, Roger Byrne, Pat Crerand, George Best, Bobby Charlton, Tommy Taylor and Denis Law, with Dennis Viollet as reserve. Since Busby made that selection, one or two other choice players have graced the colours of what has become the world's most famous team. They include Cantona and Giggs, Robson and Wilkins, Yorke, Cole and Hughes – and, of course, van Nistelrooy, Ronaldo and Rooney. Could Cheeky Charlie still make such an XI today? It would be a rash judge who left him out.

Certainly, Matt Busby recognised that here was a player able to deliver his vision of entertaining, free-scoring football. Manchester United were nothing if not goal-hungry. In the first season they finished runners-up, they scored more goals than any other team – even the champions, Liverpool. And Mitten reckoned to be up with the leading scorers every time – often 25 a season, to Stan Pearson's 30, Rowley's 40 and Morris's 30-odd. That strike-rate continued to the end of the decade, although such adventurous play meant that United often conceded what would today be considered a huge number of goals – often 40 or 50 a campaign. But what was incontrovertible – even to someone like me whose loyalty lay with the Blue end of Manchester – was that week after week, the Reds playing on their rivals' Maine Road ground provided a dynamic and exhilarating spectacle. Thus was the legend of Manchester United born.

Charlie Mitten was central to that legend, but it is a place in United's history earned by total dedication, a fact not lost on Busby, which is why he came to appoint Charlie penalty-taker. From his youngest days at United, Charlie Mitten was a practice fanatic. Every training day after the regular routines were over, Mitten would always stay behind with goalkeeper Jack Crompton and practise taking every conceivable kind of dead-ball kick – which is why he always managed to make it look so effortless when he was doing it for real in matches.

'Jack and I would stay behind at least two or three times a week – our half-hour sessions would go on for an hour and a half, maybe two hours. Jack never complained. We'd be kicking the ball around the goal, practising scoring goals, taking free-kicks and penalties, techniques for putting pace and direction on the ball. With Jack in goal, we'd spend a good half-hour on one specific kick – like penalties. And then I'd go outside the box and I'd practise from 18 yards from the edge, corner, sides of the box, typical positions from which I would always try to score in a match.

'When we were practising penalties, I'd tell Jack which side I was going to put it. I never cheated – and he still couldn't get to it. That was what I was aiming for – accuracy with power. No goalkeeper in the world should ever be able to save a penalty if the ball is struck correctly. It's all in the mind of the player taking the kick. If you know what you're going to do and you know you are going to execute it properly, a penalty is always a certain goal. Or should be.'

Charlie Mitten agreed, of course, that it was ultimately all down to confidence – but that, he insisted, came from being deadly certain about what you were doing, with practice,

practice and more practice, so that taking a penalty became automatic. You didn't even have to think about it – except to decide in which corner to put the ball. One became a craftsman by rule, an artist by inspiration.

'Looking at the number of penalty misses by the supposedly best players in the world during World Cup shoot-outs, I just wonder how often some of those players actually practise what is, after all, the simplest kick in the whole of soccer. And the easiest. Or it should be. The same sort of practice techniques should apply to free-kicks around the box. I remember I once got one against Newcastle at Old Trafford – a free-kick outside the box. They lined up and I curled it past Jack Fairbrother, the keeper, and we won 1–0. It was something Crompo and I had been practising and practising, and it had paid off.

'The secret of kicking the ball from outside the area is that you've got to put pace on the ball; you've got to hit it correctly, or it will go over the bar – you've got to practise. You must practise. You can't just put ping on the ball and then see it sail over the bar – that's what so many players do today. They run at the ball as if it was a bag of sweets and just whack it. They don't seem to realise that if you're shooting at goal, you must hit the target or at least force the keeper to make a good save, or the free-kick is just a pass back, a dead ball. You must aim: aim always for the corners of the goal. When I was shooting, I wasn't watching the keeper. I was looking for a place, the hole, where I was going to put the ball. You've got to aim for the target, especially today, with balls so much lighter.

'I used to practise from the left side, sticking it a foot into the goal in the right, far-side netting. I used to make them practise that at Newcastle when I was manager there, and there wasn't one of them that could do it. You can kick it as hard as you like, but try keeping it a foot high as well, and aiming it. A shot like that is impossible to save – it's virtually a certain goal.

'I remember taking Chelsea to play in Scandinavia on a pre-season trip when I was a UEFA coach after I'd left Newcastle. The team was having a practice session kicking the ball around, and I took a couple of balls up the other end of the pitch and started whacking them into the far-side net, a foot off the ground. And I hung a jersey tied to the far top corner and hit it, time after time – whump, whump, whump!'

To say that the Chelsea players were impressed is perhaps an understatement. Of such things are reputations made. Busby entrusted Charlie Mitten with penalties because he could see he *meant* it when he took one. Busby had seen him practising when the player didn't need to. He was serious about his game and it paid off. His record proved that.

As ever, the secret was simple – if any young footballer was willing to listen and learn. This, then, is the simple secret from the maestro revealed to me at his home, before he died, and demonstrated with an orange on the kitchen floor: 'No one should miss from 12 yards. My long hours of practice with Jack Compton were aimed at ensuring I was ready for the easiest goal chance that comes up in a match. You aim at that stanchion in the corner of the net, and no goalkeeper, no matter how good, is going to stop it if you hit it firmly and without hesitation. It doesn't have to be hit very hard. But you must know which side, and you *never* change your mind. And never turn your back when you're placing the ball on the spot. You place the ball on the spot, step backwards three or four paces, facing the goalkeeper, so you get your run-up correct. If you turn your back, you get your run-up all over the place, because when you turn your back you're out of line and when you turn round again you've got to adjust yourself. This is very important. Then, when you hit the ball, you hit it with the instep; and you must treat that kick as if it's going to be the cleanest shot you've ever hit in your life. That's every penalty – whether it's one, two or three in a match. Head down, knee in line with the ball, follow through with the foot. You can't possibly kick the ball over the bar, or stub the ground doing it that way. It's a skill that ought to be imbued in every player. But since the Continentals started coming over here, swinging the ball with the inside and outside of the foot, we've lost more and more players who *could* learn to kick the ball properly as they try to half-master these skills.'

Charlie Mitten wouldn't claim to be perfect, although he would say he was a perfectionist, and he certainly knew his craft. Perhaps that's why Busby indulged him more than any other player. Every footballer is different to a team manager, and that was the secret of Matt Busby – he knew every player who played for Manchester United inside out. The pay-off was on play-day.

'I remember many times I deserved a good kick up the backside and all he'd say was, "Well, there's always next week, son." And when the next week came, and I'd probably scored a goal, or a penalty, done something decent in the game, he'd say, "I told you, son, well done!" It gradually escalates and escalates, so that you know your boss is behind you, building your confidence. Suddenly, there wasn't anyone in the world I couldn't beat or try it on with or have a go at. The secret of Matt Busby wasn't his technical knowledge but his personal knowledge of his own players. Getting to know them was to get the best out of them.'

Charlie regularly used to cut it fine, arriving in the dressing-room before kick-off where the rest of the team would be already half-changed for the game. But Matt always knew where his Cheeky Charlie had been – having a quick couple of bob on the afternoon's dogs, his other great passion. Matt knew his flying winger wasn't in a pub or having a crafty last fag – he never drank or smoked. Then Mitten would breeze in, irrepressibly chirpy, with the usual story about an unreliable car or his wife needing help with the shopping. A poker-faced Matt would merely nod in his direction and remark casually, 'Good to see you, son.' He knew Charlie would be changed and ready to go out on the pitch five minutes before everyone else. And so did the rest of the team.

Such camaraderie was all part of the mystique without which no club ever rises above the ordinary, although Charlie insisted he was just one in a team of giant talents. After a 5–2 win against Huddersfield, one report said that the whole United forward line operated 'with superb speed and understanding . . . and the faultless timing of marionettes'.

One lifelong fan can actually remember the game which Mitten believed was the turning-point – the day a promising team finally clicked. Eric Gordon, who became editor of the *Camden New Journal* group in north London, was a 16-year-old football fan whose loyalties were more or less evenly divided between City and United, who, of course, were sharing Maine Road at the time. It was the season United won the FA Cup, and Burnley, newly promoted and having a great season in the top flight, were the fall-guys. The score sheet read: Rowley, 3; Mitten, 2.

'I was standing on the terraces, a kid of 15 or 16, getting drenched – it was pouring down, and the pitch was an absolute quagmire. As I recall, United had been playing quite indifferently. But, on that particular day, there was a sudden transformation which has always stuck in my mind the whole of my life. They won 5–0, and there was an enormous gap between the two teams. It was the first time, as far as I can remember, that United had won so convincingly. Burnley were at the top of the table and a very good team, but United's passing was just magnificent. I can still clearly see in my mind's eye Johnny Morris and Delaney on the right, with Mitten down the left-wing.

'What I can still associate with Mitten is a sense of power and precision, and a compactness that was very neat, explosive, being chased by people trying to catch him. He was well fed by Pearson and Cockburn, and he never wasted a ball. Morris was very mercurial, which was why, as a kid, I liked him. But you felt Mitten and Rowley were the two men of power. It was the worst day I'd ever spent at a football match – because of the weather – and that's cemented it in my memory. United won so convincingly that I felt something clicked, although as a kid I don't know whether I actually worked it all out, that here was going to be a great team. But I have always felt, "I saw them change!" In succeeding games, it was obvious – and you could trace it back to that particular game. I wasn't a 100 per cent United fan, but after that day I started to gravitate towards them, although I didn't actually become a follower until I'd left Manchester a couple of years later.'

It was the beginning of the eclipse of Manchester City and the arrival of the glory boys in red. This was where the legend started, with a whole team committed to attacking football, scoring goals and entertaining the public, Charlie thought. 'You had to hand it to United, they were an extremely efficient outfit, from the chairman down to the most junior lad on the ground staff. They built a football empire at Old Trafford and, of course, one that became a tremendous financial success. The lesson for other clubs is that Manchester United showed how a modern club can be created, and a mystique sustained so that it is self-perpetuating. Only the Munich air crash delayed the European Cup coming to Old Trafford. This is important, because Matt Busby realised earlier than most that soccer was not just a British preserve but a game that belonged to the world.'

Part of that world vision was taking the club game to an international audience. And so it was that United in 1950 embarked on what was their pioneering foreign tour to the United States to showcase English soccer, of course, but more importantly to promote Manchester United. Indeed, the club informed the FA that its players should not be considered for the World Cup finals in South America, the first time England had entered. It is not fanciful to suggest that the England team could have – should have? – included no fewer than six United players: Aston, Cockburn, Pearson, Rowley (already England regulars), Chilton (who later won two caps) and, of course, Charlie Mitten.

As it was, Aston was allowed to join the England squad as United swashbuckled their way across America winning eight of their twelve games, including a 9–2 win against the American national team that so sensationally put England out of the World Cup, drawing two, and losing only twice – on both occasions to the touring English FA XI.

The American tour was an enormous success and helped create something which neither Busby nor the United board could have foreseen. The tour games and the exploits of the Manchester team on and off the field were widely reported in the press in both the United States and, more importantly, Britain. The players were guests of honour and fêted wherever they went across the States; they met, mingled and were photographed with celebrities and stars, and there were first-person accounts in the newspapers from the players themselves, who were as star-struck as any terrace fan at the glitz and glamour they encountered.

John Carey, for example, filed a series of articles, including a colourful account of the team's visit to the MGM studios in Hollywood, where they found themselves guests of honour at a lunch in the stars' restaurant. Throughout the meal, they literally rubbed shoulders with and even exchanged pleasantries with half a dozen box-office stars with whom everyone back home would have been familiar – Clark Gable, Esther Williams, Arlene Dahl, Ann Dvorak. Carey could scarcely contain his sense of awe at being in the presence of this galaxy of stars of the silver screen: 'How wonderful this was to us, accustomed as we were to having the spotlight focused on ourselves so frequently! . . . The restaurant was just like any other – except that our fellow-diners were celebrated [sic] people. We hardly ate anything, so engrossed were we all in "spotting the stars" . . . Ricardo Montalban, who made a great hit with Esther Williams in *Neptune's Daughter*, spoke with us for a long while . . . and Miss Sarah Churchill was at the head of our table . . . We kept seeing many familiar faces whose names we could not recall – we could not keep pace. One of these fellows came over to us and Allen Chilton told him he had "hissed" many times because of his villainous deeds on the films. "Sure," he replied, "I'm always the dirty dog, but it's a living!" . . . Clark Gable came striding in and hung his Stetson on top of my cap! Ladies, I may tell you that he looks as handsome off screen as on it; and I don't say that because he was courteous enough to come over to our table and bid us welcome to MGM and hope we would have a good time in Hollywood.'

If today that might seem incredibly gauche, one has to remember the powerful pull cinema exerted on audiences worldwide in the days before widespread television. And here were a bunch of athletes few had heard of, hobnobbing with the denizens of the dream factory. A discussion of the mass psychology of stardom is beyond the scope of this essay but here, surely, was a clear case of acquired glamour by association. And for soccer fans, the elemental social predisposition to identify with family, clan, tribe and country found a new focus: there was a loyalty transfer, which created synthetic 'belonging' – to a football club. It was not contingent on geographical proximity: they had fans all over Britain. In the mid-1950s, Manchester United became the first club in any country to attract a worldwide following. Arguably, it was the US trip which metamorphosed United into something more than just another English provincial football team. The press ran with the story, discovering the first 'Busby Babes' in the 1951–52 season, a fairy tale that was anointed by tragedy six years later at Munich airport.

Of course, none of the team guessed what Manchester

United was to become. For most, if not all, the trip had merely been the adventure of a lifetime. And it was at the end of that tour, while the team were relaxing in their New York hotel, that the telephone call came that was to change Charlie Mitten's life.

# 7

# Road to El Dorado

You'd better go, or you'll die wondering.

Matt Busby, New York, 1950

WHEN THE UNITED PLAYERS READ THE RESULT OF THE England v. America World Cup game in 1950, they were at a baseball match in New York. The newspapers were full of America's 1–0 victory and, like aficionados around the world, Charlie Mitten and the rest of the team thought there'd been a misprint – it was obviously 10–0 to England. After all, only a matter of weeks before, Manchester United had taken on the United States team and won 9–2, and Charlie hadn't given much for their chances in the Jules Rimet play-offs.

'I'll always remember the match because the full-back against me was wearing a hairnet. I took a penalty, banged it in and it rolled out the back because they hadn't tacked the nets down properly. And this guy with the hairnet says to me, "That doesn't count, Charlie, the ball's got to stay in the net." I said, "You read the papers tomorrow." We thought, "The Americans don't even know the rules, and yet they go and beat England 1–0!" The United players were all on standby, but England had big names like Mortensen and Finney. It was a good side on paper – God knows how they lost. It was like the Bermuda Triangle! I don't think it would have happened if England had fielded groups of players from the same club – to give them three hard-core bastions of established players who knew each other. They probably wouldn't have even needed a goalkeeper.'

Conspicuously absent from England's line-up was Neil Franklin. England's first-choice centre-half had taken off on the road to El Dorado in South America. The significance of Franklin's gold-plated contract with Bogotá Santa Fé hadn't been lost on the United players. Their groundbreaking tour had blazed a trail across America and exposed them to riches and a level of affluence they'd only previously dreamed about. Fame they had in abundance; fortune, no. Mitten was absolutely clear that the US tour crystallised the career options he felt were facing him. He'd hit the headlines as never before – including virtual eulogies for scoring two penalties in United's 4–0 crushing of the Swedish World Cup squad. Yet there seemed nothing he could do as an individual to materially change his prospects for the better.

'We enjoyed the tour; it was an exciting new adventure. We'd crossed the Atlantic on the *Queen Mary*, played in Chicago, St Louis, New York, Los Angeles, and got a taste for the high life. They looked after us well, and we often drove around in huge cars. The press had been full of it when Neil Franklin and George Mountford signed for Bogotá Santa Fé. I thought: a £5,000 contract, plus £35 win bonuses – what the hell are we doing here! We'd toured the United States, beaten their best teams, yet we'd nowt in the bank to show for it. We all felt this way.'

All this was to change with the telephone call Mitten got on the eve of the United squad's departure for home on the *Queen Mary*. As in many of the best detective thrillers set in the Big Apple, the call came like a bolt from the blue while Charlie was holed up in his hotel room off Times Square.

'It was Neil Franklin. With him, he said was the Santa Fé president, Luis Robledo – the man who'd signed Neil and Mountford – would I have a word with him? Robledo said he was looking for the best left-winger in the world and Franklin had given him my name. I said, "That's very flattering, Mr Robledo. What have you got to tell me?" Robledo said, "The offer's the same as the others – would you like to come down and have a look at us?" I said, "How do I get there?" He said, "We'll arrange it – an air ticket will be waiting downstairs in the foyer for you tomorrow morning. Just make your way down here, and we'll pick you up at the airport in Bogotá."'

These days, when we take millionaire soccer stars for granted, it's perhaps difficult to understand how players like Mitten felt about the meagre prospects facing the brightest and the best 50 years ago. Today, any Manchester United player could go out and buy a new family car for cash. In 1950, none could even dream about doing that with a second-hand banger, even though a new car cost only around £100. Players like Mitten were acutely conscious that their skills were generating immense riches for their clubs but that they were being denied a fair share of that wealth and that most of them could only dream of doing anything about it.

What was on offer once they disembarked from the *Queen Mary* back in England? A wage of £10 to £12 a week. OK, it wasn't bad pay compared to a factory worker – Mitten's father was only earning £4 or £5 a week at Metro Vickers. But Charlie Mitten regarded himself as more than an artisan; he was an accomplished performer at the top of his profession who had to take a part-time job to provide a decent living for his family. As he recalled, his evening coaching sessions at schools and boys clubs around Manchester could double his week's wages. But every Saturday, United's home games were attracting anywhere between 65,000 and 80,000 fans. The terraces were literally overflowing.

'We got our biggest gate, about 85,000, for a New Year

game with Arsenal, and I had to say, "Excuse me, could you move back so I can take this corner kick?" People would be sitting on the barriers and spilling over on to the touchline. The club could have afforded to pay us more. We got 67,000 in a cup match against Yeovil. At two bob [10p] a time, it wasn't too bad, was it? They weren't short of a bob or two. United were making a fortune.'

Now, a man Charlie Mitten had never met was making him the kind of offer they'd all marvelled at when Franklin and Mountford were reported to have decamped to South America only weeks earlier.

'Robledo said there would be a £5,000 signing-on fee – the same as George and Neil – plus the bonuses and £5,000-a-year salary. The beauty of it was that I was getting half straight away. I could send it home to Britain along with a percentage of my monthly salary in sterling via the bank. I don't think there was one United player who wouldn't have gone if they'd got the call from Colombia. What else had they to play for back home? So I told Robledo, yes, I'd like to have a look.'

The exact figure had never been confirmed before this book's first publication. Everything that appeared in the press at the time was pure speculation because none of the Bogotá Bandits revealed the precise details of the Santa Fé package – except to hint that it was five figures.

Charlie knew in his heart that he had to seize his chance. Now he had to break the news to Matt Busby – no easy matter. The problem was, of course, that Manchester United regarded Charlie Mitten as their chattel. To be sure, his contract had expired at the end of the 1949–50 season, but Busby was fully expecting the player – like every other member of the United team – to re-sign for 1950–51. Under the retain-and-transfer system, a player had no choice, and Matt Busby was in no position to vary the terms of these employment arrangements.

Charlie remembered almost verbatim the conversation he

had with Matt Busby that evening in their New York hotel: 'I went down the corridor and knocked on Matt's door to tell him. He was very angry and upset. He said, "You can't do that! You're not allowed to!" I said, "I can, my contract has expired." He said, "It doesn't matter, we're going to re-sign you when we get home." I said, "You didn't tell me that before we left." There was just the assumption that we would sign as usual and do what the club said – they took us for granted. I said to Matt, "Listen, I'm 29 – not at the end of my career. Most of the team are 28 or 29, at the peak of our careers – and it's about time we started getting something out of life now."

'So he quietened down. When I told him the salary, he said, "Do they want a manager?" We had a good chat. I was always one of his favourites – we got on all right. I basically went back to what we'd said before the Cup final – that we were getting nothing out of the game. If we had to finish football right then, we'd be evacuees, or starving – we had nothing to fall back on. When we got our benefit, after tax you got about £530. That's out of £750 for five years' service. You couldn't even buy a house. What United should have done was give us the house we were living in; that would have been something.

'I said, "Look, I'm an international player. You know what we've won, but we've got nothing. And you've got nothing for being a successful manager! I'm going to Colombia to have a look, anyway. If I don't like it, I'll come back and sign for you." He said, "OK. You'd better go, or you'll die wondering."'

Busby had in fact recently signed a new £3,250 a year contract. But what concerned him that evening in New York was that he was about to lose one of his best players and that there was nothing he could do about it. What really irked him was the fact that his authority was being challenged – and that, in Busby's eyes, was the biggest sin, as Charlie was to find out a year later. But at that moment, it was clear that even Cheeky Charlie was overawed by the magnitude of the course he was embarking on. Certainly, it would have been easier if another United player had been going with him. They all discussed it. Henry Cockburn was Charlie's room-mate – and he recalled the left-winger asking him if he was interested in flying down with him to check out Bogotá. 'But I turned it down. I didn't think I was ready to take that step,' he admitted candidly, later in life. Charlie was on his own.

'So I went. I packed my trunk and arranged for Stan Pearson to take it back to England, and I took my hand luggage and flew down to South America. They were waiting for me on the tarmac at the airport – Neil and George and their wives and kids and Luis Robledo. I had a chat with Robledo and took a liking to him straight away. George had told me he was a topper, one of the best. And I did find he was a perfect gentleman. I trained with the club, took a medical and signed a contract. Air fares for me and my family were paid in full.'

Three days later, Charlie flew back to England to discuss the deal with his wife, who knew nothing about her husband's 'fact-finding' trip to Bogotá apart from what she'd read in the papers. But she had been preparing the family for the adventure of a lifetime. As he'd promised, Charlie went straight to Old Trafford to tell the United manager of his decision. Their meeting was cool, correct and formal. Busby, too, was nothing if not a gentleman. He congratulated his left-wing star and wished him every success, but there was little warmth in his words. There was no attempt to change Charlie's mind, and the FA didn't make any approach to try to stop him. His teammates all discreetly wished him good luck; some even hinted that they, too, would go if they got the call. But on the day Mitten and family left town, there was only one person at the old London Road railway station (now Manchester Piccadilly) to wish them bon voyage – the Union's ever-faithful Billy Meredith. The *Manchester Evening News* reported that Meredith had dashed the length of the platform as the train was leaving to shake Mitten's hand and tell him: 'If there had been chances like this

when I was a young footballer, I'd have walked to Bogotá.'
Mitten knew exactly what he meant.

'Any player in the land would have gone if offered such an
opportunity. Even Stan Matthews was interested in playing
out there. He wasn't too old; he always kept himself very fit.
He would have filled the place. He could have done it, he was
playing so well. I thought surely this is the start of players'
freedom of contract – the players I've left behind will not be
satisfied when they know what is available elsewhere; they
won't be happy about that. It's only a question of extending it
further. But the Players Union wasn't very strong at that time.
I thought: I'm 29, and if I play until I'm 35 at United, I'm still
in the same mess pot – I'm not going anywhere. All I'm doing
is helping to win something for Manchester United. We are
not getting our just rewards.'

# 8

# Beautiful Dreamers

Nationalism is an infantile disease, the measles of mankind.

Albert Einstein

IT'S BEEN A RIOT OF ATTACKING PLAY, A VERITABLE GOAL-FEST OF exuberant football. Now in the dying minutes of extra time in the 2010 World Cup finals, England, trailing San Marino 3–4, are under another wave of attacks. Both Marino strikers, Hidetoshi Nakata and Sun Jihai, are looking for a match-clinching hat-trick, and it seems nothing can stop them. Suddenly, England's Wayne Rooney sweeps in to block a Nakata shot on the edge of the box. In one effortless move, the power-playmaker threads a pass to Pierre Webo just inside the centre circle. The Cameroonian spins, turns and accelerates in one move, skipping two sliding tackles from centre-backs Jock MacTaggart and Darby O'Gill, and arcs through a flighted 25-yard pass. The ball is hanging invitingly on the edge of the box as England's spring-heeled Ji-sung Park strikes. The South Korean-born winger uncoils one of those prodigious leaps which have destroyed the tallest defences in the world to nod the ball down into the path of the Chilean-born Simon O'Higgins. The volley from 12 yards is unstoppable. It's a penalty shoot-out.

111

A fanciful dream? Maybe. But is it just possible that one day, sooner than we think, all players will be able to turn out not only for any club in the world, but any country as well, rather than merely the birthplace of their forefathers? Charlie Mitten believed it could come to this – and the game would be none the worse. It's already happening. As long ago as 1931, Bradford Park Avenue's John Parris was capped for Wales against Northern Ireland. Parris was born in Pwllmeyric, South Wales, of West Indian parents. He was the League's first black player, also later turning out for Bournemouth, Luton and Northampton. In 1953, Livingstone Eves was the Chile goalkeeper whose deflection gave England a 2–1 victory over the South Americans. He was born of Scottish parents. In the 1995 season, the Brazilian Luiz Oliveira, signed by Anderlecht when he was 15, played for Belgium. And to cite just one Euro 96 example: Switzerland's Kubilay Turkyilmaz, born of Turkish parents, was 'naturalised' at the age of 20. As Wembley match commentator Kevin Keegan remarked, 'You need four languages to speak to this Swiss side.'

Southampton's Matt Le Tissier could theoretically have been capped by any of the home international teams because he was born in the Channel Islands. And until the Bosman case, UEFA rules allowed players magically to lose their foreigner status in Euro competitions after becoming 'assimilated' over five years as a resident in England – or Wales or Scotland or Northern Ireland. Should Dwight Yorke and more recently Robbie Earle have opted for England rather than their West Indies alma mater? Will a player's birthplace really matter in the future? The current FIFA rule is that a player may be picked for his adopted country if he hasn't already played in his mother country's senior or Under-21 team. Is the day coming when the principle is player's choice first? And might there even be inter-country 'transfers'?

What began on the road to Bogotá in 1950 has its

counterpoint in the cases of Kingsby in 1912, Eastham in 1963, and 1995's landmark judgment won by Jean-Marc Bosman. The Belgian footballer went to court when his club, RFC Liege, cut his wages and placed an absurdly high transfer fee on his head after he sought a move to Dunkerque in France. Eastham established a player's right to sign for any league club once his contract had expired. The European Court of Justice ruling on Bosman extended that principle across the European Union. The court swept away restrictions on the number of 'foreign' players a club can field in UEFA competitions, something Charlie Mitten had long thought was inevitable.

'You can see how absurd this rule was when you look at Manchester United's position in 1994 – Wales, Ireland and Scotland were ruled as different countries in European competitions, and their players counted under the three-foreigners rule. United were unable to field a full-strength side. What utter rubbish! Football is a universal game, the European Cup is won by the best team – so why shouldn't that team have seven or eight players from different countries? We're talking about the integration of nations for peace. What more could you do than through football? Treat any football team just as a team – black, white, green or yellow – no matter where it's based. It doesn't matter which country. If someone can play football, it doesn't matter who they are, they should be allowed to play for any team they wish. On a European scale, freedom of contract in one country should be welcomed across the continent. There should be no restrictions on who can play for which team, in any country. This should be applied by FIFA all over the world. We could do with some of these foreigners' skills, and they could come here and learn some of our steel. Their skills would rub off on us and, of course, would improve the game, and in ten years we might start producing more than just a few first-class players. After all, the most important people in the game are those who are paying to watch the game. They want to be entertained.'

This was the authentic voice of the Bogotá Bandit speaking. The football internationalist, careless of political boundaries, was concerned only for the development of the beautiful game as the pre-eminent sporting spectacle on the planet and for its practitioners to be free to parade their skills in any arena, anywhere in the world, for any team. Real Madrid showed the way in 1956 when they lifted the first European Cup, with the likes of di Stefano and Rial (Argentina), Santamaria (Uruguay), Torres (Portugal) and Kopa (France) in their side. That same season, Accrington Stanley in the Third Division North several times fielded 11 foreigners – all Scotsmen. In season 1993–94, Dundee United fielded 11 players born outside the UK. In 1995, Ipswich could pick a complete first team of players classed as foreigners: Forest and Yallop (Canada), Paz (Uruguay), Williams (Wales), Wark and Mathie (Scotland), Thomsen (Denmark), Norfolk (New Zealand), Guenchev (Bulgaria), N. Gregory (Zambia) and Tarico (Argentina). In season 1995–96, half a dozen Premiership sides were almost there: West Ham (8), Leeds (6), and Bolton, Chelsea, Coventry, Everton and QPR all with five so-called 'foreign legionnaires'. And at the start of the 2005–06 season, Arsenal fielded a first team without an English-born player, while Chelsea could certainly put out a first XI full of *gastarbeiter* players any week and still look invincible.

'Manchester United, Eintracht Frankfurt, Nottingham Forest, Real Madrid; it doesn't matter who, they should be able to, if they think it's in the interests of their fans and the way to success. We want to see the best teams playing at our grounds on Saturday afternoons. I'm interested in the game of football, in skills and artistry.'

Just as Bogotá Santa Fé were in 1950. And if nationality is no bar at club level, could it not ultimately become irrelevant for international games – as Colombia's national FA showed in

1950? Within weeks of the 1995 Bosman ruling, a score of South American footballers were reported to be seeking Spanish nationality 'to improve their career prospects'. Argentinians, Colombians, Uruguayans, to be sure. And once 'naturalised', they would be eligible to play for Spain at international level – as Alfredo di Stefano did more than 50 years ago.

So what's in a nationality? Any nation-state is merely a geographical expression – most obviously in the case of the United States of America, which is a patchwork quilt of cultures united by a common dream. Certainly, for the beautiful dreamers of the Bogotá episode all those years ago, it didn't mean very much. The supreme irony is that what Charlie Mitten and Luis Robledo began in banditry could prove to be the visionary first steps to the way the beautiful game will be globally organised in the future.

The two men couldn't have been more different: Charlie Mitten, penniless athlete, a gladiatorial fugitive from the last vestiges of English feudalism who had come in search of El Dorado; and Luis Robledo, the wealthy cosmopolitan at ease in the capitals of the world.

Robledo was the son of a Colombian millionaire cattle baron. After being educated in England at Downside and Cambridge, he joined his country's diplomatic corps, becoming first secretary at the Colombian embassy in London. He later went on to become the Colombian ambassador to the EEC and died in Bogotá in 1987. He first hit the headlines in 1948 at the age of 24, when it was revealed that he had been secretly married for more than 18 months to the 37-year-old daughter of an English earl. Lady Bridgett Poulett, debutante of her year, had been the darling of the smart set in the 1930s and variously described in the gossip columns as 'glamorous . . . decorative . . . streamlined . . . lively . . . lovely . . . and sought-after'. She even made the headlines when a friend's flat was robbed of jewellery. In August 1939, she put Morecambe on the high-society map when she opened the Middleton Tower holiday camp in the Lancashire seaside resort. News of her clandestine tryst broke when it was reported that she had been caught up in riots in the Colombian capital while on a secret visit to her in-laws.

Unorthodox marriages were something of a tradition in the Poulett family: Lady Bridgett's father had married a Gaiety Girl after a whirlwind romance in 1908, and her brother married an actress in 1933. The reason she gave at the time for keeping her marriage a secret was 'the general rule against diplomats marrying nationals of the country to which they are credited'. To keep up the pretence, she and her husband lived in separate flats until their secret was discovered. By all accounts, she was an adventurous woman and played a key part in her husband's raid on English football. She personally liaised with Neil Franklin and George Mountford, making all their travel arrangements, and provided clandestine stopover accommodation at her London flat for the footballers' families on the way out to Colombia.

Robledo himself had been a keen polo and football player in his younger days and an avid supporter of Arsenal. The red and white colours of Bogotá Santa Fé were modelled on the Highbury club's strip. This was the soccer fanatic who saw an ideal opportunity to indulge his enthusiasm for the beautiful game when the Dimayor breakaway 'super' league was set up in Colombia in 1950. The country had been importing players from all over South America since the Colombian league was set up in 1948. The Dimayor row saw the country banished from FIFA, just as the world spotlight turned on South America, then hosting the competition for the Jules Rimet trophy. As Charlie recalled: 'Football was a big thing with Robledo, and he realised that to get in and play against these countries would bring prestige to Colombia and also be a financial success for the club. The continent was football mad. Bullfighting had been the big spectacle but football was completely taking over.'

Robledo was in a unique position: he had a soccer dream and the money to realise it – the creation of a football super-team from scratch, made up of the greatest players in the world, nationality irrelevant. He was, in fact, the first exponent of the make-believe newspaper-reader diversion 'fantasy football' – only he was doing it for real. In men like Charlie Mitten, he found footballing freebooters who wanted to play at the highest level for the greatest reward. Thus two dreams coincided to produce one brief season of heaven on earth for both.

The metaphor has an impeccable pedigree. Thus, if Jesus Christ were to come to Liverpool, they'd tell you on Merseyside throughout the 1960s, Bill Shankly would move St John to inside-right. More pertinently for our tale, it was Spain's own soccer visionary, Santiago Bernabéu, who once offered Matt Busby 'heaven on earth' – to take over as manager of Real Madrid. It was after the Spanish team had overwhelmed United's Busby Babes in their first European Cup foray in 1956. Busby's rejoinder was that heaven *and* earth were both in Manchester. More interestingly, Busby is said to have told one Madrid player who urged him to give up Manchester that if Real gave him (Busby) di Stefano and Hector Rial, United would win every trophy in the world.

Amen to that, Mitten said. But when he turned down Real Madrid after Robledo's personal dream fell apart, it would perhaps not be stretching things to say that Cheeky Charlie did indeed miss the boat to paradise.

# 9

# Bandit Days

Give him the ball, and you could relax as he did the
business. Around the penalty area, he had the deadliest
left-foot shot.

Neil Franklin, Stoke City and England, on Charlie Mitten

*LA VIOLENCIA* WAS IN FULL SWING WHEN THE MITTEN FAMILY
stepped on to the tarmac at Bogotá airport one July day in
1950. It was to prove the bloodiest outbreak of civil disorder
to have disfigured the country since independence. Charlie
Mitten didn't know it at the time, but he was soon to find out
that he had walked into a revolution off the soccer field as well
as on it.

The Republic of Colombia, occupying 440,000 square
miles on the north-eastern tip of South America, was founded
in 1819 as a result of a revolt in the Spanish colonial vice-
royalty of New Granada, which then included modern-day
Colombia, Venezuela, Ecuador and Panama. Its first president
was the independence leader Simón Bolívar. In 1830,
Venezuela and Ecuador seceded, to be followed in 1903 by
Panama. But Colombia's often-hailed 'model democracy' was
shattered by civil war between 1899 and 1902 in which more

than 150,000 people died. Even after peace was patched up, the political consensus between the Conservative and Liberal parties remained fragile. The assassination in 1948 of leftist Liberal leader Jorge Eliécer Gaitán saw simmering social discontent flare into *La Violencia*, characterised by outbreaks of violent civil disorder on the streets of the big towns and a state of near anarchy in some parts of the countryside. It was to continue unabated for 20 years, and 300,000 people would die as a result. This was the country to which Mitten had come to seek a better life. The root cause of the trouble was, of course, the vast disparity in wealth between the rich and the poor, something which immediately struck home with Charlie.

'We found that the country had a huge social divide: there was the great mass of poor people, and above them a tremendously wealthy millionaire elite, mostly descended from the Spanish conquistadors, who in fact owned the country. And here we were, English footballers, pioneers – that's how we regarded ourselves – the first rebels against a restrictive and archaic system which treated its principal characters as second-class citizens, mixing freely with this upper class. We very quickly found that we were accepted into the inner circles of Colombian social life. As a professional footballer, I rubbed shoulders with oil barons, wealthy landowners and cattle ranchers and their cohorts.'

The foreign stars of Santa Fé and Millonarios found themselves fêted by the wealthiest sections of society, and living virtually the same lifestyle. As promised by Luis Robledo when they'd discussed terms on Charlie's flying visit, a palatial, hacienda-style house was put at his family's disposal. It had four bedrooms and a magnificent enclosed garden. And they could afford to pay for servants, a maid and a gardener to take over all the household chores, although Charlie was glad his wife insisted on supervising the cooking.

'You got paid every month, no problem. If Luis Robledo

promised you something, you got it. I lived like a millionaire for the year I was there – there's no doubt about it. We found we adapted very quickly to this way of life. There was a large expatriate English community in Colombia and a splendid and well-manned consulate which ensured that the English way of life and public holidays and so on were not forgotten.

'So what with the incessant Colombian festive days – rarely a week went by without at least a couple of big fiestas – my three children [John was nine, Charles, jun., seven, and Susan, a toddler of three] have never forgotten Bogotá. It was a year-long holiday in the sun for them. My most used suit – my dinner suit – was on my back four nights a week for receptions, parties and all kinds of functions. We were invited everywhere. Soccer was regarded as a profession in Colombia, and we players were treated as heroes, like lord mayors!'

The biggest problems initially were getting to grips with the language and finding adequate schooling for the children. But the Mittens soon made firm friends among the expatriate English community, two in particular being an English tutor, Ossie Pope, and author Chris Dixon, who wrote a definitive book, *Green Fire*, about the emerald-mining business in Colombia. (The country is the world's biggest producer of the precious stones.) The children coped much better than their parents with learning another language.

'From my two sons' point of view, the language barrier was broken down by football. They would go out and play on a piece of waste ground outside our house, coats going down for goalposts and boisterous teams soon made up with the local kids. This led to many tea parties with neighbours, and so John and Charles soon developed a good Spanish vocabulary. My wife, however, found things rather more difficult with the shopping, a particular chore, and fortunately she was able to entrust most of it to our *muchacha* [servant girl].

'Life was certainly kind to us. The Colombians in general liked English people, and we made many friends. We had a reputation for keeping our word, and that went a long way with them. Bogotá even then was a big modern city with department stores, cinemas and office blocks. And although the cost of living was perhaps double what it was in Britain then, we still lived very well since I was earning five times more than I did with Manchester United.'

But if the English footballers were so obviously ostentatiously welcomed by the country's elite, their affluence in the midst of so much poverty did not seem to engender any feelings of ill-will among the mass of the ordinary people. Mitten and his compatriots were household names and most people knew them by sight because they were followed by press photographers everywhere they went. (That celebrity cut no ice with the police, however. Within weeks of their arrival, Franklin and Mountford were arrested for failing to carry ID cards, a requirement of the martial law regulations.)

The only occasion on which Charlie had recourse to the police was within weeks of the family's arrival, when the Mittens' new Ford Sedan car was stolen. 'George Mountford and I had gone down to the club offices one afternoon to see Luis Robledo, and we'd parked the car outside. We were in for about an hour, and when we returned, we found an empty space. At first I thought I'd forgotten where I'd parked it. Then it hit me – it'd been stolen. We reported it, and the usual police dragnet was thrown out. It was found two days later in an orange grove, propped up on blocks of wood on its axles, minus wheels, radio, tool kit, windscreen wipers – almost every removable part. Even the cigarette lighter had been taken.

'Fortunately it was insured, but I remember the police inspector telling me, "Charlie, if you want those things back which were stolen from the car, you can go to the local market and buy them all back tomorrow." Some people were so poor, it was their way of life. It was quite common to be driving through Bogotá in the evening just as it was getting dark and feel a terrific bump under the car. The wheel had caught in an open manhole in the middle of the road. The local Indians had a favourite trick of stealing manhole covers and melting them down to make iron gates and all sorts of other utensils to sell in the marketplace.'

But never at any time did the soccer exiles or their families feel threatened or in danger from the incipient unrest which within months of their returning to Britain would break out into sustained and horrendous years of blood-letting, even though the signs of what was to come were all around, as Charlie recalled. The most obvious was the curfew. Although there was plenty of nightlife, with many clubs and bars, the streets of the capital were largely deserted after 9 p.m.

'Bogotá was quite a political hotbed at that time, and even during the day your car would be halted at checkpoints manned by soldiers in pillboxes every few miles on all roads in and out of the city. They would check who you were, what you were doing driving in that area, and check that the car had not been stolen – and that we were not carrying firearms.'

The guest players, especially the Englishmen, became well known to fans – and police – within weeks of them starting to play with their new club. The football-crazy citizens of Bogotá treated the English stars with the kind of adulation usually accorded to pop stars.

'Within a few games, you'd have thought we were gods – tin gods – which was ironic given England's performance in the World Cup that summer. I was a household name within weeks, and I couldn't walk down the street without being stopped by well-wishers. All the shops would be trying to outdo each other in giving us discounts, and we got invited to every function going. Looking back, it's hard to believe it all now.'

In fact, Charlie found the biggest danger to him physically actually came from hostility on the pitch – as he discovered in the historic game against Uruguay, played within weeks of his arrival at Bogotá Santa Fé. The Colombian FA thought it would be a spectacular coup merely to play the new world champions and arranged the exhibition match before the Uruguayan World Cup squad had dispersed. The scratch Colombian team included Santa Fé's two English imports plus Charlie's inside-left partner, Hector Rial, and their goalkeeper, Chamorro – the best goalkeeper Mitten ever saw anywhere in the world – both of whom were Argentinians. From Bogotá rivals Millonarios came another Argentine, centre-forward Alfredo di Stefano. Charlie recalled the capital was 'steaming' with excitement the day the Uruguayan team flew into Bogotá, fully expecting a stroll.

'They swaggered into town, very aggressive, as if to say, "This is how we're going to play the game." The ground was packed, and it turned out to be a heck of a game, very tough and no prisoners taken. I had grazes all down my thighs and backside. They didn't like getting beaten, and only afterwards realised that Colombia had as good players as they did. It has always struck me since that if you put 11 footballers together, irrespective of race, colour or creed – or language – they'll all want to beat the other 11 players, whether individually or by team play. We found at Santa Fé with our team of many nationalities that we could make ourselves understood on the field quite easily. Soccer has a language of its own among players.'

Di Stefano scored twice, one of which came from a Mitten cross, and Rial got the third in Colombia's 3–1 victory.

'Uruguay realised at half-time that they had a match on their hands. This was the arrival of South America's exuberant technical skills on the world stage. For us to beat the world champions was no fluke – you might sneak one goal, but not three. South American football had arrived but very few people in England realised it.'

Mitten and di Stefano kept in touch for years afterwards, and Charlie would often joke that if they had played together more often, the Great Alfredo would have scored so many more goals! Cheek of a truly stratospheric kind. But, it seems, not at all out of order. As the man they came to call the 'White Arrow' put it: 'I saw Charlie Mitten play many times in Colombia, and he never made it easy for his opponents. Internationally, he was one of the best I've seen, intelligent and creative, and he never wasted a pass. The ball always went to where he placed it, he was so accurate. He was an excellent player.'

Mitten's wing-play soon made an impression in the Dimayor league and Charlie found himself a firm favourite with the fans – and the target of opposing defences. The league then consisted of 20 teams including the two Bogotá sides, Santa Fé and Millonarios, who shared the magnificent 35,000-seater, municipally owned stadium in the capital. Charlie's team proved to be very successful, and he recalled the £35 win bonus was bankable as regular income. The stadium amenities were far ahead of anything in the English League at that time, with catering and toilet facilities that would have put most First Division grounds to shame. English League facilities have, of course, improved dramatically since then, but Charlie reflected that even then, so-called backward soccer nations like Colombia treated their fans as honoured guests rather than a swinish herd as too many British clubs seemed to do.

It was in this appreciative setting that the adventurous play and sharp shooting of *El Char-lez* won a fanatical following.

'Hector Rial told me after about three weeks or so, that *I* was a favourite because the crowd would break out into singing all sorts of Spanish love songs when I'd scored a goal or done something like that. And I didn't know what the hell they were singing for. And Rial would say, "*Char-lez*, they are singing for you." And I'd say, "What, to string me up?"'

Once on the pitch, Mitten became literally untouchable. It always amused him to recall that on the rare occasions when he was caught by a fierce tackle, there'd be a pitch invasion. Once, he had to go off with an injured thigh, but so incensed was the crowd that the offending player was withdrawn too – for his own safety. In fact, to make a big impression as soon as possible had been Charlie's game plan. Having brought his family halfway across the world, and with no experience of foreign climes, he felt he dared not fail.

'When my wife and I had talked about me going to Colombia, I'd said I'd go and turn it on as soon as I got there. That I would really play. No one loves a duff foreigner. I'd wear their colours, just drop into their ways, get acclimatised, learn the language and try and absorb being one of them in the first two or three months, because that's the quickest way to get friendships going and earn respect. Which I did. I joined in all the larks with my new teammates, and I think I was a success. I was confident that I was the best left-winger in Colombia at that time, and I always, in every game, tried to play as if I was. I made goals and I scored goals. I really enjoyed setting up the local lads – and the fans, of course, would love it when their lads got on the score sheet. And if I felt I could score, I'd have a go – but I'd never waste a shot from an impossible angle. If I wasn't almost certain of scoring, I'd always square the ball back.'

Neil Franklin rated Charlie Mitten as highly as his old Stoke City teammate Stanley Matthews. In March 1949, just 12 months before Franklin decamped to Bogotá, his Stoke City side had run into the United whirlwind in a league game in Manchester, losing 3–0. 'Stoke Dazzled by Mitten' was the post-match headline. The *Sunday Dispatch* report described Charlie as the best uncapped outside-left in the country: 'Mitten's brilliant footwork ran full-back Watkins dizzy . . . Franklin and goalkeeper Herod were towers of strength . . . but the feature of the game was the Mitten fireworks . . . scintillating dribbles . . . and an unstoppable drive for the third goal.'

Franklin told me shortly before he died in 1996: 'Charlie

was a very sharp ball-player and fast off the mark. If they were in trouble in defence, Charlie would drop right back into his own half screaming for the short ball – Stan used to do the same for us on the right – then he'd be away! You could stand back and relax as he did the business. He just loved to have the ball. And once he got around the penalty area, he had the deadliest left-foot shot.'

Such skills made an indelible impression among the fans and won Charlie a devoted following. The most colourful memories he had of his year in South American football arose out of the fans' wildly partisan behaviour. Most incidents involved one of the English referee corps, specially imported by the Colombian FA, who considered them the best in the world. But that reputation did not provide much protection when things got over-enthusiastic. Referees always had a police escort on to the pitch and back to the dressing-room at the final whistle. And even then their safety couldn't be guaranteed. Charlie never forgot one particular incident involving Tom Pounder, a referee very popular with the English players. Charlie lodged with Pounder for a time towards the end of his contract, after his wife had left for England, and they became good friends.

'I think at the time we were playing in Cúcuta, which is coffee-and-banana country. We'd scored a first goal which we knew had been a shade offside, and Tom Pounder had given it. There was uproar as he was surrounded by the opposing players protesting and jostling him – he didn't so much walk from the goalmouth to the centre spot as be carried in the mêlée. Tom was very worried and asked me, "What shall I do?" I said, "Go and see the linesman and ask him, *si gola or no gola*?" So Tom goes over to the Spanish linesman, and *all* the players follow him to hear the verdict. Tom asks him, "*Si gola or no*?" The linesman says, "*Si gola!*" And immediately all the players set about the linesman and left Tom alone. The game was restarted with difficulty.

'At the end of the match, we are in the dressing-room after getting changed, waiting for Tom Pounder, who was due to fly back to Bogotá with us. We go outside to the gates, and still there was no sign of Tom. So I went back to the dressing-rooms with George Mountford to look for him. When we went into his changing-room, we found him laid out on the floor. Well, we bring him round and ask him what happened. And he says, "One of those b*****d gendarmes hit me with his rifle butt!" It appears that one of his escorts that day had been a keen home supporter – and had just clocked him with the rifle and shut the door. We used to have a great laugh about it later, but at the time it really shocked Tom – and he wasn't one who got upset easily. I think he came to the conclusion that he wasn't temperamentally suited to the Colombians' hot-blooded style of play. Tom was a very nice chap on and off the field.'

Charlie also recalled Pounder telling him of another hair-raising incident involving their capital rivals Millonarios. It was a needle match between the Bogotá club who were then top of the league and rivals who were near the bottom. Millonarios, despite home advantage, were heading towards a goalless draw with just about five minutes to go when the underdogs were awarded a free-kick just outside their opponents' penalty area. The visitors' centre-forward took a long run and belted the ball hard towards goal. Unluckily for Pounder, the ball struck him on the back and was deflected into the Millonarios net. According to the laws of the game, there was only one possible decision the referee could give – a goal.

'When he signalled a score, that's when the fun started. The angry Millonarios crowd swarmed on to the pitch and joined the players in a free-for-all. It took the intervention of a platoon of militia to quell the riot and restore enough order for the remaining few minutes to be played out. When Tom finally blew for full time, the top of the league side had been beaten by the bottom club and the crowd turned their spleen on the luckless official. A cloud of missiles rained down on him as he and the players made their way to the dressing-rooms, chaperoned by a squad of militiamen. But the changing-rooms provided no relief and baying crowds of fans laid siege around the door, demanding blood and worse.

'The crowd refused to disperse, despite the direst warning of action by the military, but the truth was they hadn't got the numbers or resolve to carry it out. Tom was effectively trapped, barricaded in his dressing-room. Finally, an armoured car was brought from the nearby barracks and Tom hustled away – for all the world like a notorious criminal. We used to have a good laugh about such incidents later, but at the time they were anything but funny.'

There were, in fact, six English referees operating in Colombia at that time, and another of them, Bill Brewer, also provided a fund of similar stories. Charlie related how in one game in which Brewer gave a decision against one of their opponents, the player had bent down, swiftly picked up a clod of mud, and hurled it at the referee.

'For a few seconds, anything could have happened as players of both teams circled over to where the ref stood. Then, ever so slowly, Brewer, with a fierce glint in his eye, blasted his whistle, halting the game. Everyone froze. Then he deliberately bent down, picked up an equally generous clump of mud and threw it smack into the offending player's face. I couldn't believe my eyes and was expecting all hell to break loose.

'But, no. What happened was that the shocked footballer ran as if his life depended on it, 25 yards into the centre of the pitch away from Brewer. Not another played moved; all were waiting to see what was going to happen next. Brewer didn't gave them time to think – he immediately blew for the game to restart with a free-kick, and got not one iota of trouble throughout the rest of the game. What sort of uproar would such an action cause in England today, I wonder.'

The fact was that with first-class soccer in its infancy in Colombia at the time, the authorities were trying to get some sort of discipline into the game – hence the English referees. But sometimes it seemed that the fans were trying to outdo even *La Violencia*. On yet another occasion, Pounder recalled blowing his whistle for the two captains to come to the centre circle for the pre-match toss-up. The coin was flipped, but before he could blow for the game to begin, the home captain, jogging back to line up, pulled a small knife out of his sleeve and hissed under his breath, 'We win or else!' It turned out to be idle bravado, but it had Tom Pounder watching his back throughout the game – and, by the end, looking forward to his own final whistle!

'They should have been on danger money – the referees were the real pioneers. They did an excellent job of establishing discipline in Colombian football. There were certain elements out there who would try virtually anything to make sure their side won. Tom Pounder told us he was once offered £180 to fix one of our games. Needless to say, he turned it down flat – and I was very happy to score a vital goal by which we drew 1–1, one of twenty-four that I scored in Colombian soccer.

'There was a more amusing incident when I took a penalty once. I stepped back – I never looked at a goalkeeper; I always knew where I was going to put it. I put down the ball, step back and, as I run up, I have to stop because the keeper is standing a yard in front of the ball. So I turn to the referee, who started laughing, and say, "Is this catch as catch can? Right, we'll start again." I bend down, put the ball on the spot and straight away, without stepping back, I bang it into the back of the net. The crowd roared. They loved it.'

Charlie's bandit days were not all about playing football and scoring goals. The players' training regime wasn't particularly arduous, and the English players always found they had plenty of free time on their hands. Colombia is a big and beautiful country, and the Mitten family took the opportunity to tour the sights and see as much of the country's breathtaking scenery as they could.

And it was on such a day trip that Cheeky Charlie Mitten had his closest brush with disaster during the whole of the Colombian escapade.

# 10

# Paradise Lost

Come with us, Charlie, there's no money in English
football.

Hector Rial, Bogotá, 1951

A GIANT STATUE OF CHRIST STANDS A SILENT SENTINEL ATOP
the very brink of the soaring falls of Tequendama, two hours'
drive from Bogotá City. In the rainy season, its flashing silver
streams cascade down a drop of 135 m (440 ft) and overlook a
magnificent rock wall cirque which is often shrouded in mist.
The Mitten family regarded it as one of the most beautiful
places they ever visited in Colombia. No wonder trips to the
'hot country' were among their favourite jaunts. And, yes, the
Mittens visited 'El Dorado', too – Lake Guatavita, the
epicentre of the legend whose origins are based on the story
of a shooting star which fell to earth and gave rise to the cult
of the man made of gold.

The myth of El Dorado – the Golden Man – grew out of
the Conquistador quest for the native Indians' secret
goldmines and even a fabled lost city of gold. The mountain
basin in which Bogotá is situated was once inhabited by the
most advanced pre-Colombian culture, the Muisca Indians,

133

who almost certainly followed a god-man cult which was the basis of the El Dorado legend. It was next to Bacata, the Muisca capital, that the Spanish settlement of Santa Fé was set up in 1538, and which soon became a staging-post for the great quest.

One of the main targets of expeditions was to track down the mysterious lake of gold, in which the Muisca high priest, smeared in gold dust, washed himself every morning while his people threw in gold artefacts in worship of the Sun God. And so was discovered Guatavita Lake, a unique, almost perfectly circular geophysical feature north-east of Bogotá, believed to have been formed by a meteorite strike in pre-history. Identified as the place where the ancient ritual was said to have taken place, it became the main focus for the quest as well as a tourist attraction for visitors like the Mittens.

Colombia's mixed population, which in 1950 was around 27 million and today numbers some 43 million, traces its roots back to indigenous Indians, Spanish colonists and black African slaves. The most numerous racial grouping, the *mestizos*, are of Spanish–Indian descent and make up 60 per cent of the population. After Bogotá, the biggest towns are Medellín, Cali, Bucaramanga, Manizales, Cúcuta, Cartagena, and the beautiful coastal city of Barranquilla. Given the size of the country and its geography, Charlie's team, Santa Fé, travelled to all away matches by plane, with an often hair-raising coach ride to finish the journey from the airport at the other end.

'Routine air travel for our team was one of the immediate differences between the Colombian league and England, and it took some getting used to. It would have been impossible to get to some places otherwise, of course. It was while playing with Santa Fé that I first appreciated the tremendous value of air travel. When I was back in England, I never ceased to be astonished at the fuss in the press when we flew our Newcastle United team to a league match. The great majority of professional footballers in this country would much prefer a quick trip home on a Saturday evening after a game rather than a night in a hotel followed by a tedious rail journey on the Sunday. I can foresee the day when all the top teams will land directly at football grounds where they are due to play that same afternoon.'

Medellín was one of Santa Fé's big away games. In the days before that city became the world's clearing house for the processing and shipment of cocaine, it was, Charlie recalled, a cotton and silk town, the size of Harrogate or maybe Birmingham, with broad, palm tree-lined avenues. The large all-seater stadium, a replica of the one in the capital, could hold 35,000 on vast, tiered galleries of concrete bench seating which ringed the ground in continuous banked lines. It never rained, and the crowds would bring their own cushions, thronging to games that were fiercely fought – but with goals rather than guns.

The Englishman's play was appreciated because he seemed to lack none of the ball skills of the Colombian players. And, in the cantinas and restaurants, errant soccer players were unlikely to be the target of assassins. In 1994, nine days after returning home from the World Cup, Colombia's own-goal scorer, Andreas Escobar, was gunned down as he left a restaurant in Medellín by three men obscenely shouting 'Goal!' as they repeatedly shot him. His murder provoked national outrage and 100,000 weeping mourners cried 'Justice!' as they filed past his open coffin at the funeral. In June 1995, Humberto Muñoz Castro was convicted of Escobar's murder and given a 43-year jail sentence, later reduced to 26 years. He was released for good behaviour in 2005.

Charlie could recall nothing like the Escobar outrage happening in 1950: 'The fans were very partisan and you had to watch which side of the stadium you sat at, but there was none of this kind of violence. They came to enjoy themselves and watch us turn it on,' Charlie remarked ruefully.

League matches were played on Saturday afternoons at 3 p.m., with regular training on Tuesdays and Fridays. The rest of the time, players were free to do as they pleased, and Charlie made the most of it, especially as he was able to afford a decent car, a Ford Sedan de luxe. Many people later asked him what it had been like in Colombia, and Charlie's reply was always unambiguous. 'I can honestly say we led a wonderful life. Often we would spend a day at Bogotá's superbly situated golf course and magnificent country club, with its stained-glass windows and inlaid wooden floors, boating lake, roller-skating drome and archery range. There were facilities for horseracing and a playground with slides and swings for the children. All this and the sun always shone. You might occasionally get a few minutes' downpour, but you could guarantee that the sun would be shining as brightly as ever immediately after.'

Bogotá, at 2,640 m (8,660 ft) up in the central highlands, is the third-highest capital city in South America. The country is split by three Andean mountain chains, or *cordilleras*, running north–south, with a flat coastal region to the west bordering the Pacific, and to the eastern interior, wide *ilanos* or plains. The climate is tropical on the coast and in the west, cooler in the highlands. 'The difference in altitude was very noticeable as you travelled through different parts of the country,' Charlie recalled. 'It took me three weeks to get my altitude lungs, but our cars never did.'

Charlie and George Mountford became quite good golfers – perhaps, Charlie believed, because of the thin air, in which they found they could drive the ball well over 300 yards with ease. The two families would also often spend a day with cattle-rancher friends out in the *ilanos*, going horse riding with the children and having great fun on the donkeys, or would simply drive out of Bogotá and picnic amid ravishing scenery.

They became very friendly with an English girl who had married a Colombian and regularly visited them at their home in Santandercito, about 20 miles from Bogotá. It was set amid orange and grapefruit groves, coffee and banana plantations, and fabulous wild orchids which would have sold for a couple of hundred pounds in New York or London. Their friends' hacienda (ranch house) would be an oasis of tranquillity, with servants in attendance as they strolled the orange groves or lounged around in bathing-trunks. After a late-afternoon ride around the estate, they'd return to the ranch house for a delicious meal Colombian-style with plenty of game meat, followed, of course, by the country's after-dinner speciality – coffee. The owners could reach out and take their own coffee beans off the trees, let them ripen for a few days and then make delicious coffee.

'It was a wonderfully relaxing life for us. We could turn the kiddies loose and know they would be all right climbing the trees, riding the donkeys, eating oranges and bananas until they looked like them. Santandercito was an amazing change in such a short time – from the cement jungle of Bogotá to the lush jungle vegetation around the hacienda. It took us about an hour to drive. Gradually, as we descended, it would get warmer as we neared the coffee plantation. We would spend all day with our friends there. Cool streams watered the groves and plantations, and we always used to remark about this wonderful sight that it was just as it was the day the Lord made it.'

But to get to this paradise they had to drive over narrow mountain roads which descended steeply by several thousand feet in only a few miles. On one side of the road was a drop of thousands of feet, on the other, the towering Andes. And if there was a cloudburst, tons of earth and rock from the mountainside could block the way for hours. It was on one such trip that Charlie got the biggest fright of his Colombian adventure. It was a fine, sunny day and the road was clear, but it was a close-run thing.

'Coming down the steep mountain road one day, the brakes

on our car failed. The sudden change in altitude had affected the oil level in the compression system, and you can imagine my horror as we rushed downwards along this narrow road and nothing was happening as I pumped the brakes. Fortunately, as it was a brand-new car, the handbrake was working perfectly, and I managed to pull the car up with it. Then it was just a case of waiting a little while for the oil pressure to build up again before we continued our journey. It certainly taught us a lesson, and we always treated the steep roads with the greatest respect after that.'

Back at the training camp, Charlie Mitten was treating the footballing skills of his Latin-American hosts with equal respect. They were to serve him in good stead, in a glorious swansong to his playing career, when he returned to England.

The essential difference in the training regime which immediately struck him was the emphasis on ball work. Training was supervised by a German coach who found it difficult to implement a strictly fitness-based curriculum, especially among the native Colombian players. Charlie noted that they seemed to find it far easier to drink a bottle of wine than take part in a brisk session of purely physical exertion. But although they were never enthusiastic about doing laps around the pitch, put a ball at their feet and they would gallop around all day.

'This was the thing that hit you most forcefully – they all just loved to have the ball. Our coach seemed unable to handle the South Americans in the side, so we received little tactical instruction. But with a team of such first-class performers, we found we could make it up as we went along. The number-one thing I saw in South America was that they learned first to become the absolute master of the ball. Every footballer there was a ball-player – there wasn't a kick-and-rush player in the country. Of course, some footballers are better ball-players than others, but *all* could trap a ball, kill it dead with a flick of the foot. All could pull the ball on their thigh or on their chest – and after that, they all knew what to do with it.'

The main, unstated, tactical difference was something Charlie soon picked up on. In his first few games for Santa Fé, he would attack in the style he had been deploying in English soccer – going up to the full-back, beating him and then clipping the ball up across the goalmouth for a header. But it soon became clear that the South American players were averse to heading the ball. They advised Charlie, when he got past the full-back, to run to the line and put his pass back along the ground so they could side-foot it into the net.

A low cross struck hard and back from the dead-ball line is a devastatingly difficult ploy to counter, and Charlie took the lesson to heart. Later, he would introduce the tactic at Newcastle, and was surprised at how many orthodox English defences could be wrong-footed by it.

'It was an entirely different type of game out there. It was a short-passing game – ten-yard passes all the time – with more activity on the run of the game inasmuch as you constantly had to hold on to the ball, pass, then move into position for the return. It got rather comical, really. When I did lay on the low pass from the wing to provide the goal scored with the inside of the foot, the South American players thought this was marvellous and would carry me half the length of the field to celebrate the goal.

'A side-light to this was that George Mountford used to score a lot of goals with his head because he would be the only one of our players going up to head the ball in the goalmouth. In every country I played, I learned something about the game and kept it for use at a future date. Although the tactics of foreign sides then were not entirely suited to the faster, more rugged and hard-tackling English League soccer, there were certain aspects that could have been incorporated much earlier. It was one of the faults of the English game that for so many years it has ignored developments in soccer elsewhere.'

Another novelty Charlie encountered was the goalkeeper's throw-out to set up an instant attack from the wings, which was developed in to a fine art. The Continentals picked it up and were doing it for years before it caught on in England. One of the few English exponents – considered an oddity at the time – was Frank Swift, who died in the Munich air crash. Now, of course, it is part of the repertoire of every goalkeeper. In fact, the big kick, Charlie found, was alien to Colombian football.

'The longest kicks in were corner-kicks and dead-ball kicks – from static positions. But even then, quite often, the ball would be played away short. The emphasis all the time was on control of the ball, that is, having possession as well as mastery of it. And when they had it, could they kick it! There was, for instance, some fantastic overhead kicking and double kicking of the kind which shook British fans when they saw the Hungarians trounce England at Wembley in 1953.'

And, one might add, who can forget the dazzling 'scorpion' double-heel goal-line clearance by the Colombian goalkeeper René Higuita in the Wembley game against England in 1995? Charlie would have said that's what the fans pay good money to come and see; they want to be entertained by skill no matter how eccentrically executed. Those terrace depressives who dismiss such artists as flashy and big-headed, he believed, are only a tiny minority. But it is a ghost that hasn't been completely laid to rest.

'I think the reason why the South Americans became so much better ball-players than their counterparts in England is because English players after the war did not take enough pride in themselves to become better ball-players. They never thought, for instance, of pulling a ball down onto the thigh – nowadays more players are doing it. It was a question, perhaps, of English players thinking [that performing] such tricks with the ball was showing off. In England, players have tended to be too modest about such ability and just tried to get on with the job. Even today, you will hear fans shout "Big-head!" if a player tries something adventurous in control techniques.'

Charlie thought the ridiculous thing about all of this was that English players could have been doing such feats of ball control 40 years earlier. 'As the years rolled by, the science of football in England has been sacrificed to the god of speed. For too long, managers have tended to look only for the following abilities in players: (1) speed; (2) endurance; (3) ability to get the ball in the net as often and as quickly as possible. All good qualities in a footballer, admittedly, but not at the expense of ball-playing ability and a keen sense of positional play.

'I felt my time in Bogotá improved my football: the close passing, looking for the spaces, the falling-back funnel system of defence, the supreme ball control these South Americans had, bringing every part of their body into use to control the ball. There was a common fallacy in English soccer at the time that the South Americans couldn't shoot – well, we've seen what nonsense that was. We all know now just how fantastic their shooting ability is – on the volley, on the turn, from every possible angle and range.'

Among the exponents of such artistry were, of course, di Stefano and Charlie's inside-left at Santa Fé, Hector Rial. Charlie recalled him as a 'brilliant' ball-player. And, indeed, Manchester United fans were later able to judge for themselves when Rial came to Old Trafford with Real Madrid.

It was the second leg of United's first foray in the European Cup, and the Manchester team were trailing 5–1 from the first game in Madrid. Under Old Trafford's first floodlit match in Europe, Real had raced to a two-goal lead thanks to the artistry of Rial and Raymond Kopa. To their credit, the Reds fought back to level it by the end of a pulsating game, but went out on aggregate. Few doubted that United had been vanquished by the best team in the world. But Charlie, with fearless objectivity, always rated his old United inside-man Stan Pearson better than Rial, talented though the South American was.

This is not to say the Colombian sides were a pushover. Their style of play may have been different, the pace not as rushed but, as Charlie recalled: 'There were no easy rides. The Colombian league teams were all hard to beat – especially clubs like Millonarios, Cúcuta and Barranquilla. You had to nail them down first and feel your way a bit. We didn't cruise in any of our matches.'

The Colombian league took its football seriously, especially the two Bogotá teams who regarded themselves as the new soccer elite who would show the world what the country could do. So while there was exuberance in coaching and training, and even a degree of indulgence when it came to preparing for matches, discipline was strict. With all league matches played on Sunday afternoons, most of Santa Fé's away matches involved overnight stays, with departure from Bogotá the day before. Charlie found it amusing when the younger players found their freedom curtailed.

'We'd start out for away games travelling on the Saturday afternoon by plane – trains didn't go to many places – fly to the local airport and then, if necessary, finish off the journey by coach. From Saturday morning, the players had to report for what the club called "concentration", which meant being under the supervision of the coach. To keep the younger lads away from temptations like girls, they were kept in quarantine! It was well known that they'd think nothing of being out with a girl an hour before kick-off if they could get away with it.'

One of the away-match destinations Charlie especially recalled was the trip to Cúcuta, about 45 minutes' flying time from Bogotá in the 'hot country'. A bus met the Santa Fé team party at the local airport for the drive to their hotel along a narrow, steeply descending mountain road. It was the only other time in South America that Charlie felt like saying his prayers.

'The bus driver, obviously a Cúcuta supporter, drove like a maniac down the mountain road, which was a track only about one-and-a-half vehicles wide. So a vehicle coming from the other direction created quite a problem. That short drive put years on me. George and I held on to our seats for dear life, quite expecting any moment that we would be hurled over the side of the road to our death, thousands of feet down the mountainside. There was no such thing as a Highway Code, and drivers in Colombia drove on the horn: hoot as loudly as possible and tear around corners, hoping that nothing was coming in the opposite direction! A short time after we came back to England, we read of a terrible accident between two buses on this road to Cúcuta. They had met head-on and crashed over the sheer drop at the edge of the road. Obviously neither driver would give way.'

George Mountford had signed his contract with Santa Fé a couple of months before Charlie, so it finished earlier, and he and his family left to return to England. Their friendship had grown both on and off the field and Charlie admitted that he felt at quite a loss when George left Bogotá, even though he was living with some English friends. Homesickness was a real and depressing problem.

'George and I had become very good pals and our wives were good friends, too. When we visited each other's homes in Bogotá, the kettle was always on, and it was just like a little bit of England in South America. George had been a really good player with Santa Fé – quick and always after goals. But he had been a bit unfortunate with injuries, which seemed to take a long time to heal out there. But I'm sure he never had any regrets about making the trip.'

Neither, of course, did Charlie. And it wasn't just because of the football or the money – although it was the cash that enabled him to indulge himself in what became an unforgettable experience that many dream of but which few ever get the chance to make come true – owning a racehorse.

Bogotá had a modern racecourse, and Charlie, not an infrequent patron of the sport of kings, had often wondered what it would feel like to be punting on his own horse's nose. He decided to find out. At the city's January bloodstock sales, he bought a two-year-old filly which he named after his daughter. Susanna Muchacha (Susan, servant girl) cost £1,000 and, after a couple of trial outings, went on to win several races and provide a reasonable return in winnings for her owner. Before Charlie returned home he even got his money back by selling the horse at the same price he'd bought her for to a stud-farm owner who was impressed not only by her form, but also by Susanna Muchacha's impeccable English pedigree – out of Derby winner Trigo!

Charlie was remarkably blasé about his six months as a racehorse owner – a rare if not unique distinction among pre-contract-revolution soccer stars. What he remembered most fondly was visiting the horse at its stables. 'I must say it gave me a lot of pleasure watching her race in my colours: orange and grey quarters and orange cap. I whiled away many an hour watching the filly in trial runs and often used to bring her carrots at the stable. In the week that I arrived back in England from Bogotá, Susanna Muchacha won the local fillies classic race for her new owner.'

Missing a major purse on the turf was as nothing compared to the glittering prospect Charlie Mitten let slip when he decided to quit Bogotá and come home. In the last few months of his contract, it had become obvious that his wife had been feeling particularly homesick, and she and Charlie had been concerned for their children's education. They'd been unable to find an English school and felt that they would get a better education back in Britain. Charlie had more or less resigned himself to returning to England.

Ironically, Robledo's dream had suffered a blow just as

Charlie was arriving, when Neil Franklin had cut short his contract and gone home early. Sadly for Franklin and his family, the culture shock had proved too great: they had been unable to adapt to local customs and found the language too great a barrier to overcome. (In later years, however, Franklin was to claim that the flight to Bogotá had in fact been the only way he could get away from Stoke City, as we shall see in Chapter 17.) This reverse defection shocked the urbane Robledo, who was 'indignant at Franklin's contempt'. As Charlie recalled, the whole episode created a lot of ill-feeling in Bogotá.

'Santa Fé officials were furious when news reached Bogotá that Franklin had returned to England. There were some hard things said to George Mountford and myself about Englishmen breaking their word. For weeks afterwards, private detectives followed us around everywhere, obviously checking up that we weren't going to leave town. Even the British consul was concerned and asked whether we were happy in Bogotá and whether we intended to honour our contracts. He said British prestige was at stake.'

But Charlie was determined to see out his contract. Months later, when his wife decided to return to England ahead of him, the club rewarded his good faith by paying for first-class passage for them back to England aboard a cruise liner sailing from the port of Barranquilla on the north-west coast. They even paid for a week's holiday for all the family in the resort before the liner sailed.

Colombia was eventually to reapply and be readmitted to FIFA on the condition that all foreign players be sent home, and time was called on Luis Robledo's dream. 'Santa Fé collapsed and Robledo resigned. He'd put in an awful lot of money. He deserved better than that,' recalled Charlie.

But as one man's dream crumbled, another visionary was evaluating Bogotá's wealth of soccer talent and hoping to build another. Santiago Bernabéu was a Spanish lawyer and former footballer who had spent years organising a public subscription to realise his ambition of building in Madrid the most modern football stadium in the world. Now he wanted a team that could do justice to the new arena and was recruiting the best players in the world for a team called Real Madrid. To his eternal regret, Charlie failed to take the bait.

'Bernabéu flew to Bogotá to discuss signing three of us – di Stefano, Rial and myself. We had dinner and we discussed terms: he was offering £10,000 a year, plus £10,000 signing-on and a three-year contract. Plus bonuses. I thought it would be a good move for me. We could have had a lovely house in Spain. But when I discussed it with my wife, she said she wanted to stay in England, and we were both worried about the children's schooling. She said that when she'd got back to England, she hadn't been able to get a house because we didn't know where I'd be playing or for whom. If only I'd known . . . I found Bernabéu, like Robledo, a charming man, but there seemed to be more steel about Bernabéu, less of the dilettante. Turning him down was folly for me, a mistake, because I suppose I could have had some European Cup medals. Alfredo and Rial did all right – they became part of the Real side which dominated European football for ten years. And I suppose there would have been that chance for me too. Rial urged me to go. I recall his exact words: he said, "Why don't you come too, *Char-lez*, there is no money in the game in England." In 1952, Real Madrid could easily have afforded the fee Fulham paid United for me. They paid £20,000 each for Rial and di Stefano.

'So I could have gone to Real. I realise now what a big mistake it was to turn them down. It's the only thing I regret in my life. Real Madrid was a replica of what Matt first did at United, getting seven or eight good players together. Real had them – players like di Stefano, Puskas, Kopa, Mateos, Santamaria, Rial and Gento, who was on the left-wing, where I might have been.'

Francisco Gento was undoubtedly one of the most devastating left-wingers in the history of the game. He had an absolutely explosive turn of speed and a ferocious left-foot shot which, when on target, was virtually unstoppable. But as right full-back Jimmy Armfield proved when England surprisingly beat a di Stefano-led Spain 4–2 at Wembley in 1960, he could be played by astute positioning. Indeed, it was the only way – and Armfield can justly claim the duel between the two on that day was an honourable draw. Certainly, if you gave Gento even an inch-wide opening, he was uncatchable. It was a match in which England raised their game sufficiently to neutralise the skills of di Stefano, who, on the day, was often scintillating but never totally dominating, as he skipped over the quagmire of Wembley's rain-lashed pitch while many of his teammates floundered. I know, because I was there, a schoolboy huddled high on the terraces, marvelling at the White Arrow's ability to literally walk on water.

Charlie had a somewhat different opinion of the Spaniards' flying left-winger: 'Gento was a speed merchant. He had pace and a tremendous shot, but he wasn't very subtle. Alfredo later used to say to me, "*Negative, negative*, no football brain." But he could run, all right. Di Stefano would say, "I have to play two games of football: I have to play for Gento and for myself – I have to tell him where to go and where I'm going to put the ball." But Gento was a good player for the team because you need pace on the wings. If you've got good ball control, all the rest are extras – a good shot, a football brain, pinpoint passing – but you must have pace. Gento had it. If he got away from you, you could never catch him. I'd like to think I'd have brought a little more thought to the Real left flank.'

Di Stefano himself believes it would have been a close-run thing between the two players because Gento was ten years younger and a shade faster: 'Once Gento came, it would have been difficult for Charlie because Gento was one of Real's best players. And at that time, there were a lot of international players who wanted to come to Madrid. But with his ability, I feel Charlie could have played. It was very painful for him when Real became famous and to know that he missed playing for such a great team.'

Of such stuff are the great 'what-ifs' made. No one – and certainly not Cheeky Charlie Mitten, as he freely admitted – could have guessed that Bernabéu's dream wasn't going to be as ephemeral as Robledo's.

'At the time, no one had heard of the Spanish side. With the benefit of hindsight, I could have been part of another legendary team. But I did at least have the pleasure of playing with one of the world's greatest footballers – Alfredo di Stefano. You wouldn't think it just to look at him. The Maestro was balding early on and started losing his hair in his 20s. He always looked a bit like an old man – but what a player! Looking back on my career in football, I would say there were two players above all others I've seen who had the unique ability to make players around them play – di Stefano and Ian St John. They were master playmakers. Di Stefano didn't have a shot, but he could score goals. He scored a hat-trick in the best game I've ever seen – the 1960 European Cup final between Real Madrid and Eintracht at Hampden Park when Real won 7–3. He was absolutely immaculate. I had the whole match on film as an instructional film for when I was coaching.'

Di Stefano was aided and abetted by Puskas, playing in his first final, who scored all four other goals. Eintracht were no pushovers, having beaten Rangers 12–4 on aggregate in the semi-final. But the German side were mesmerised by a virtuoso performance from Real's two apparently ageless masters, both of whom were 33. Real went on to become kings of the world by beating the South American side Penarol in the first World Club championship.

The wheel had come full circle. South American flair having inspired Continental soccer, a Continental club studded with South Americans had returned the compliment. But ten years earlier, another soccer pioneer, having come to the cradle of the exciting new footballing style, was returning to tell all he knew. It is clear that at least part of the reason why Mitten turned down Real Madrid was that he really believed the soccer establishment in England would forgive him his transgression, marvel at the wonders he had seen and, above all, listen to what he had to say.

He was to be bitterly disappointed. And it was while he was facing the wrath of the godfathers of England's football establishment that he suddenly wished he'd brought back the gruesome trophy of a real bloodletting that he'd been given in Bogotá.

# 11

# Facing the Firing-squad

Hello, Mitten. I see you've caused us some trouble.
Fred Howarth, Football League secretary, 1951

THE ONE THING CHARLIE MITTEN DIDN'T BRING BACK FROM
Bogotá was the bull's ears. Memories, a bagful of new tricks
and a healthy tan, yes. But the bull's ears, no. Even Cheeky
Charlie found them in poor taste. They were, in fact,
presented to him as a mark of respect by a soccer-mad
matador right after he'd killed the bull in front of Charlie's
eyes. And the eyes of 60,000 screaming aficionados of the
*corrida*. The whole Santa Fé team had been special guests of
this particular matador – and, of course, his theatrical
dedication and the final *coup de grâce* had brought the house
down. It was the English soccer heroes who were expected to
receive the trophy honours. Charlie recalled: 'It was
gruesome, but not a souvenir I could refuse.'

The reason was that bullfighting was still a popular
spectacle – like cockfighting – and visiting matadors from
Spain were the highlight of the bullfighting season. Charlie
was astonished to be told by one bullfighter that he was paid
£12,000 for each *corrida* or bullfight. Of course, he could have

been indulging in a little wishful thinking. The *corrida* was very much a waning attraction. Indeed, there were no more avid soccer fans than the bullfighters themselves. 'We would go into the bullring, put our coats down and coach them in the skills of soccer. We never really asked them to reciprocate by teaching us the craft of tauromachy – we had no desire at all to meet the bulls in combat.'

Charlie reckoned the year he spent in Colombia was probably one of the last bullfighting seasons when the *corrida* was able to compete seriously with soccer as a spectacle. 'By the time I left, football had definitely taken over from bullfighting as the biggest spectator sport. It was cheaper to attend, far more of a contest, and it didn't involve killing anything . . . except the players.'

Charlie can't recall what he did with the bull's ears, but had he known his pleas were to fall on deaf ears back home, he might have saved them for the FA disciplinary committee which heard his case when he got back from Bogotá – or didn't listen to it, as Charlie later insisted. Not that he didn't have any warning of what his likely fate would be: he was still in Bogotá when, with a mixture of disgust and disbelief, he'd heard of the four-month suspension meted out to Neil Franklin.

An irate Mitten told the press: 'Franklin is not under contract with Stoke; he isn't drawing any wages; he is not allowed to train with the club. Yet the club are negotiating to sell him. Is there any other business in the world whereby a person is sold, yet is not under contract?'

And, for good measure, Mitten ridiculed Manchester United's 'wastage of postage stamps. They keep sending me 14-day suspension notices – I knew all about the suspension "racket" before I signed for Santa Fé.'

Back in Manchester, the letter columns of newspapers were a cauldron of debate over a provocative call by a correspondent signing himself 'Keen Red' for the 'sinner'

Charlie Mitten to be boycotted by fans on his return. But most readers remained unconvinced that United's roving left-winger had committed any crime. The feelings of 'Tolerant Supporter' of Wythenshawe were representative of the balance of opinion about the Bogotá Brigade: 'I read with disgust the comments by "Keen Red" about Charlie Mitten. As I see it, all the man tried to do was better himself. I must admit, I didn't agree with the way the business was gone about, but I've always maintained there are two sides to every story. The loyalty of supporters like "Keen Red", Manchester United could well do without – and a player of Charlie Mitten's calibre, they could well do with. Sorry your dreams didn't materialise, Charlie, but come back to our playing fields, lad, just come back.'

Charlie Mitten might have been acting on that one letter alone when he flew to London from Bogotá in July 1951. He wanted nothing more than to take the wing again on the wide open spaces of the English League – and for Manchester United in particular. His notoriety had, of course, preceded him, and even as the plane was taxiing to a halt on the runway at Heathrow, a sudden thought occurred to him: that he was nothing more than an actor, a supporting part, a walk-on in what now seemed like a piece of theatre. And that he was watching this character whom everyone knew as 'Cheeky Charlie' go through a performance. He couldn't believe *he* actually was the character.

What had triggered these thoughts was the announcement from the pilot over the Tannoy: 'Will everyone please remain in your seats for a moment – and let Mr Charles Mitten, the famous footballer, leave the plane first.' The reason, the pilot added, was that the world's press were waiting in the arrivals lounge to speak to him. Allowing Charlie to leave the plane first would help other passengers get through the crush more easily. Charlie recalled his overwhelming feeling: 'My face felt as red as a beetroot as I got up from my seat and walked down the aisle with everyone watching. I thought to myself what a bloody load of stupid codswallop all this is. This publicity game!'

That is not to say that Charlie Mitten, Bogotá Bandit, lately of Manchester United, hadn't courted the newspapers during his year in exile. He did, and he made no apology for it in our series of interviews. But at the time, he said, he approached the media interest from a strictly one-way perspective: he had something important to say which every reasonable person would want to hear. His flight to Bogotá had been such a momentous step that he felt compelled to seize any opportunity to explain and justify his actions as perfectly legal, wholly honourable and easily understandable. Once the issues were out, it could only benefit the profession to which he was committed: the beautiful game. Thus thought Charlie. But he soon discovered it didn't quite work like that.

It takes two to tango, and from the press point of view, 'Charlie Mitten, Soccer Outlaw' was an irresistible story first and foremost, and the symptoms of something rotten in the state of English football very much a poor second. The underlying issues of freedom of contract, the maximum wage, the whole basis on which the game was run were rarely explored to contextualise the Bogotá Brigade story. Thus the press throughout his year in exile readily provided the outlaw with a megaphone through which to shout the odds from thousands of miles away to the fans, fellow players and football authorities – and to newspaper readers. It was a year of pure theatre, a year through which the press vicariously lived the outlaw life of a brazen bandit, scarcely realising they were chronicling a revolution foretold.

But if the approach of the press was largely superficial, this was due in part to the weakness of the Players Union, and the ambivalence of many top footballers about the issues raised by Charlie Mitten's defection to Bogotá. Billy Wright, the man who was to make the England centre-half position his own, dismissed any suggestion that players were poorly paid. But, then, Wright never put a foot wrong with the authorities at either club or country level. And even Neil Franklin's reasons for defecting were at best confused.

Franklin later wrote in his autobiography, *Soccer at Home and Abroad* – apparently in explanation of his change of heart – that he believed players had no legitimate grievance over money, and that he was opposed to freedom of contract, abolition of the maximum wage and players having a share in transfer fees. Of course, such an act of contrition may have had something to do with his wanting to continue a career in soccer management, which he went on to do with Hull City, Crewe Alexandra and Stockport County. Franklin had much to offer any club. A star in the truest sense, he was a cultured centre-half. He played the defender's role in a way that was years ahead of its time in English soccer – as creatively and skilfully as an attacker. He could look after himself when it came to technical ability.

The scabrous and short-lived Union journal, *Soccer*, captured the perception of the great mass of players. It noted that football writers had for too long murmured about a rotten system, speaking only in guarded tones of its abuses and unfairness. 'Anyone who believes the system can remain if it goes on finding ways of keeping (only) the stars content – they can look after themselves – is making a grievous mistake.' Which was an accurate assessment of the likelihood of the game's top stars using their clout to change anything; most knew quite well what the score was and most were quite content to take the 'brown envelopes' and say nowt. (Charlie Mitten was adamant that never at any time during his days at United did he or any other player receive 'extra' payments.) But such divisions help explain the long years of Union weakness. Charlie Mitten was a star and he decided, like Franklin, to strike out on his own. As he was to discover, though, it didn't matter how good you were; if you rocked the boat, you were on a hiding to nothing. And when it came to a showdown with the club and soccer authorities, the gentlemen of the Fourth Estate didn't lift a finger in protest. After all, the way football was organised was like the weather – part of the natural order of things.

So flattery in the press and by journalists didn't impress Mitten much. He'd been on a learning curve, as we say today, since United's highly successful American tour, and he'd been mentally filing away his experience of the way the media worked for future reference while he got on with the one thing that really mattered to him – playing the game.

'Adulation never meant a thing to me. It always embarrassed me. I liked to let my football do the talking. But it really hit me that publicity was part of the game that day sitting in the aeroplane coming into Heathrow on the way back from Colombia. Until that moment, I was not really aware how much the press and football feed off each other. When I arrived at Fulham a few months later, I remember a young girl came down to Craven Cottage to do a publicity stunt with Johnny Haynes and myself and we had breakfast with her in the café. She was only a slip of a girl – must have been about 16 or so – and she went on to be a big star. It was Petula Clark, and I thought at the time, what the hell are you doing here, girl? Then I realised what all this was about. And I just thought, good luck to you, girl. She went on to be a great success – though, of course, I never met her again.

'There was a similar occasion while we were in America. We were sitting on the beach when along comes Burl Ives with his ukulele slung on his back, and he sat down with us. He was only a starter then, not as famous as he became. And we were chatting away, about how to sing and all that, and he said, "Why don't you boys give us a song?" So we all joined in, a publicity picture was taken and we went our separate ways again. The same thing happened when Frank Sinatra and Phil Silvers came over to the Azores.

'I suppose it was the same with the press and me at

Newcastle later – although I honestly didn't consider myself a star. The most objectionable people I've found are those who think they're something that they're not. Great people, the true stars, are very modest. They think, "I'm blessed with a gift from God of this thing I do well and it's paying off, and that's it. Leave me alone, I'm quite happy." But the press people say, "It's my job to latch on to you, to feed off you and everything you do." I suppose it's live and let live, but I did often find it difficult to take – all those people who come in and bullshit you and don't know what they're talking about. It's great when they're decent and straightforward and know what they're doing, down to earth. They're not wasting your time. If you know what you're doing, you'll be a success. I can go back and point to people I've met around the world in my lifetime and say why they were a success.'

One such person who made a big impression on Charlie was Santiago Bernabéu. When Charlie first met him, he thought the Spaniard was some sort of impresario, which, in a way, he was. A lawyer in the late 1940s, he'd single-mindedly pursued his dream, organising a public subscription to build a new stadium in Madrid. Then he'd said, well, we need a team to go with it. Charlie soon came to realise that here was a man who was in every sense a *caudillo*, a boss who meant what he said, a man who got things done.

Charlie had been puzzled how Bernabéu came to choose the Bogotá trio. He didn't think the Spaniard had seen them play. Whether he had or not, Charlie never found out. All Bernabéu cryptically told him was: 'I am trying to get the best players in the world to represent Real Madrid. I've been advised to come and see you. I've got all your records, so I don't need to see you play.'

But Charlie turned him down – no wonder it was to be his one big regret. Instead, he returned to England to face the music. And, in the absence of any others prepared to listen, he found himself having to swallow bitter medicine.

So it was that Cheeky Charlie Mitten, the Bogotá Bandit, went before the FA firing-squad during the lunch hour one July day in 1951. The first words the FA communicated to him in over a year were spoken to him as he arrived at the London hotel for the joint FA–Football League hearing: 'Hello, Mitten,' said Fred Howarth, League secretary. 'I see you've caused us some trouble.'

Charlie recalled smiling mischievously and replying: 'The Lord helps those who help themselves.'

To Charlie, the FA disciplinary tribunal which summoned him was nothing more than a kangaroo court, where a bunch of shopkeepers found their lunch hour interrupted by the chore of having to pass sentence on a naughty boy. The quicker they got it over with, the sooner they could get back to their real business. The overwhelming impression that remained in his mind was that here was a group of men who were not the slightest bit interested in football. The issue that concerned them was money. How much had Charlie made? Would it prompt other players to be less resigned to the pittance they were being paid? Something had to be done to discourage the others.

'Every question put to me at the tribunal concerned finance. How much had I made? What was my contract? What were the bonuses? I told them nothing. What business was it of theirs? The whole tone of the tribunal was that here was a thieving little boy who had to be taught a lesson. They were not interested in the style of football I'd seen, or whether there was any danger of South American football beating the English style of soccer. They never asked whether South American countries like Brazil, Uruguay or Colombia were capable of beating England in future international matches. Nothing.

'One of the biggest absurdities of the whole proceedings was one of those venerable gentlemen of the tribunal remarking to me: "Do you know you've forced Manchester

United to transfer you?" Forced them? I thought it must be very painful for United being forced to transfer me for only £22,000! Out of that, all I received was my original 1938 £20 signing-on fee.'

Those were Charlie's thoughts after the event. At the time, he didn't know that Manchester United had decided to put him on the transfer list – or, indeed, that United would not be taking him back at Old Trafford, although he admitted to me that he had an uneasy feeling it was going to happen. It was just that he didn't want to believe it. If the FA tribunal wouldn't listen, Matt Busby would. But even as the three of them – Charlie, Matt and United's secretary Walter Crickmer – trooped into the committee room, Charlie got an inkling of what was to come.

'I had Walter Crickmer on my right and Matt on my left, and me in the middle, like a convicted gangster. I told Matt and Crickmer that I had taken KC's advice, that my case was solid in law. And they said, "Oh, just let's get it over with." I can understand that attitude now, from the club's point of view. Manchester United had already made up their mind to transfer me, and they wanted the transfer fee, although I didn't know that at the time.

'So we went in. They said I had broken my contract – what had I to say about it? I said that wasn't true, because my contract had expired and I hadn't signed a new one with United. For the US tour, my contract had been in existence in May when we left on the *Queen Mary*, but it had expired while we were in the States. So the suggestion that I was still under contract when I took Robledo's phone call to discuss his South American offer was nonsense. I said I'd taken counsel's opinion that if I were to take the FA to court, I'd win my case, because this was a restriction of trade, a restraint on me lawfully contracting my labour.'

Each side might have been speaking a different language: the disciplinary committee were not in the slightest bit interested in hearing Charlie Mitten's case that the contract system was unfair – after all, the Players Union had been telling them that for half a century. They saw no reason why the system should change, any more than they should take seriously absurd suggestions that a bunch of foreigners might conceivably be able to play the game as well as Englishmen.

The committee didn't even bother to retire to consider a 'verdict'. The whole affair took less than half an hour. They banned Charlie for six months and fined him £250 – which in 1951 was the equivalent of six months' salary. Neither Busby nor Crickmer made any sort of plea on behalf of the player. The punishment was far more severe than that meted out to the Stoke City players: Neil Franklin and George Mountford had been suspended for only four months. Billy Higgins and Bobby Flavell got similar terms.

'This tribunal of nine tradesmen wanted to discipline me somehow; they were determined to make an example of me. Those nine people sitting around the table in that committee were so stupid; they refused to see that it was all going to change. I'd realised it the year before, but I couldn't wait because I was bobbing on; I was 29. Players like me couldn't afford to wait two or three or five years for them to make up their mind about giving us a proper contract, a decent deal for the future.

'They could have controlled the whole salary structure of football if they'd had the foresight, made some sort of concession. The general working man in Britain then was only earning £6 or £7 a week. But football, being a profession, should have been a free man's profession, where they made their own contracts. And it's funny how that eventually happened. It was to come up again, the same story with George Eastham, when I was manager at Newcastle.

'The press reported that I'd said the committee had been kind, and their punishment was fair – not too bad. But they made that up. I was very angry at the time, but I bit my tongue, thinking what a bloody state football is in here. The clubs can't even stand up for their own players.'

There was worse to come. There was to be no salary from United or a new contract, and the club also fined him £250 for the same offence. Charlie thought that he'd be welcomed with open arms at Old Trafford; after all, at the height of his powers, he believed he still had much to offer. Matt Busby listened politely – about the new style of soccer, the players he had seen like Rial and di Stefano – and then gave Charlie the hard word: United would not be re-signing him, and he was to be put on the transfer list. Mitten was devastated. As he told it to me, it was clear he still couldn't believe that United rejected him. It was something he'd never articulated before, and his mixed feelings betrayed his elemental love of Manchester United, which never faded.

'I told Matt he was making a big mistake – I was a better player than I'd ever been before going to Colombia. I said they could give me a month's trial, and they'd soon find out whether I was telling the truth. But it was no use. Matt was still the perfect gent, but he made it clear the board were making an example of me. Once you'd crossed Matt, you didn't come back again. Lots of players have told me that.'

If that wasn't enough, Charlie was told that he wouldn't even be allowed to train at the ground during the period of his suspension, and he saw this as petty, spiteful vindictiveness.

'I was very angry with Manchester United and didn't speak to anyone at the club for months afterwards. I thought what a clown I was to even consider coming back to United when I'd had the offer to go to Real Madrid. What a bloody clown! I could have done with an elder statesman giving me some advice. It was the turning point in my football career, but never mind. It worked out all right for me.'

And so, for the first time in his life, Charlie Mitten paid a Sunday-morning visit to the pub. But not to drown his sorrows.

# 12

# Salsa Sabbath in Salford

He was so ultra-confident, you always felt you'd be
winners.

Sir Bobby Robson, Fulham, England, Sporting Lisbon,<br>Porto, Barcelona and Newcastle

IT WAS THE LOCAL BUTCHER WHO SAVED CHARLIE MITTEN
from going mad with frustration. For a man whose life was
playing football, the prospect of six months out of the game
was truly torture. In September 1951, three months into his
ban, he was getting very itchy feet. The last time he'd kicked
a match ball had been in Bogotá four months earlier. And it
had really been in anger. For it was in this, his last match in
Colombia, that Charlie Mitten was sent off for the first time
in his career. It resulted in a two-week suspension which had
seen out his contract in South America. But on that occasion,
at least, he admitted he'd deserved the punishment.

'I was up against one lad who'd obviously been tipped off by
his manager to mark me close. Well, I'd lost him again and
had passed him at full speed when he caught me, and I went
down on the hard ground and tore the side of my leg red raw.
It was an English referee, and he blew for a foul for tripping

me. But the player was kicking me around the ankles as the free-kick was being lined up.

'So I shouted to the referee, "Don't you realise he's standing here kicking me after fouling me? He wants to be off the bloody field!" And the ref said, "You shouldn't be telling me what to do!" I was so angry – it was the only time in my life I'd lost my temper on a football field. This lad was smiling all over his face, so I grabbed his shirt and told him in no uncertain terms that I hadn't come all the way to Colombia for him to kick lumps out of me, and I pushed him backwards and he fell over.

'Well, he got up and came at me swinging, so I hit him one in the stomach, and there was a bit of a riot for a few minutes as the other players dragged us apart. We were both sent off – it was the first time in my life. I got suspended. And so I retired two weeks before the end of my contract. That was the only time I got caught by a player marking me and deliberately fouling me – fortunately!'

So here was Charlie, back in England with the season in full swing, suffering what can only be described as withdrawal symptoms. It's just the sort of situation you discuss with your friendly neighbourhood butcher. That's when he got the invitation to drop in at The Spinners Arms that Sunday morning.

'I'd called in to collect the week's meat ration at Walter Tittle's shop and got to telling him all my troubles. He listened very attentively and then asked me to come and have a kick around with his lads. I hadn't known that Walter was the secretary of The Spinners Arms, a Sunday pub team in Salford. So when he offered, I took him at his word. The really hard part of my FA punishment was not being able to play in a competitive game. I'd been keeping myself fit in the local park, but match practice is absolutely vital for any footballer to keep his game sharp. This seemed the only way.'

So it was that Charlie Mitten, England, Scotland and

Colombia international, star of Manchester United, turned out on a cinder pitch for a club on the very bottom rung of the beautiful game. From South America to a Manchester Sunday league – just for expenses. The record shows that the game at Lower Broughton – a place more unlike Bogotá it would be difficult to imagine – attracted a gate of around 200, paying precisely nothing. They saw a lightning left-winger make his way through a match in which he put three goals past 22-year-old goalkeeper Ernie Jones in The Spinners' 5–1 victory over The Papermakers Hotel. Asked later about his status as a suspended player – and an FA ban on Sunday football – by an unusually large press contingent, a jubilant Charlie, cheeky as ever, riposted: 'It's all right. In Bogotá, they go to church in the morning and a football match in the afternoon.'

Mitten's effect on the Papermakers' defence must have been much the same as Cristiano Ronaldo's on Bolton Wanderers' defence, when United's Portuguese star stepped out – or should that be introduced step-overs – for the first time in English League soccer in August 2003. Charlie, conscious of the gulf in skills, telephoned the losing team's president to commiserate. 'I told him I'd enjoyed myself and hoped I hadn't upset his team too much – I'd been grateful just to be able to play a game,' Charlie recalled.

The *Daily Mail* reported darkly that, although the game had been a friendly, 'Mitten had technically broken the rules, and it could be a matter for the FA to deal with as it raises a delicate matter of football law.'

Charlie would say the real delicate matter was whether FA rules were totally outwith the law. In the event, the FA wisely decided not to pursue the matter of Cheeky Charlie's Sunday-morning kick-arounds. But there was to be no reprieve at Old Trafford. On 7 December 1951, three weeks before his suspension was due to end, Matt Busby told Charlie that United were selling him to Fulham. The London club were reported to have paid a near-record £22,000 for his transfer. It was the worst news he'd ever had in his life. The love affair with his beloved Manchester United was over. Looking back on the episode, Charlie admitted that he had stayed in England, playing pub football, precisely because he half-believed that United would relent and take him back.

'They got the transfer money and saved six months' wages as well. I should have sat down, talked it out with my wife and gone to Real Madrid – even on a month's trial; the offer was still open. I couldn't play in Britain, but I could anywhere else. It's just one of those things that comes as an afterthought. I would have taken the FA to court if I'd had the cash, because I knew I was on to a winner. I was in the right legally and morally.'

Whether Matt Busby would have changed his mind had United been struggling is uncertain; Busby was a man who didn't like being crossed. The Scots brogue hid a steely resolve, as the independent-minded Johnny Morris found out in 1948 when he was transferred to Derby County for a new record of £25,000 despite being a member of the FA Cup-winning squad. Once Busby had grown into the job, no one challenged his authority in the dressing-room. So Matt Busby would probably not have changed his mind. As it was, United were flying high and were to end the 1951–52 season as champions for the first time in 60 years. And Busby did not relent on the training ban, so Charlie went on to play half a dozen friendly games for The Spinners. If, privately, Busby was genuinely sorry to be losing his Cheeky Charlie, precision passer and spot-kick king *extraordinaire*, he was unable (or did not want) to show it.

The same attitude prevailed at Stoke City, where the club's ruling burghers gave their rebels no second chance either. The club's board blithely cut off their nose to spite their face in refusing to re-sign Neil Franklin and George Mountford when they returned from Bogotá. At the end of that season, Stoke, having finished four points off the bottom, narrowly escaped relegation. The following season, they weren't so lucky.

In fact, the two clubs who had fallen from grace into the Second Division in 1952 were Huddersfield and . . . Fulham. But it was not for lack of effort or flair by their new signing, Charlie Mitten. Given the decline of the illustrious London club in the 1970s and 1980s before Mohamad al Fayed's cash got them into the Premiership, it's perhaps difficult to believe what an exciting place Craven Cottage was in the 1950s. In 1949, they'd been promoted to the top flight, had held their own for two seasons, and were developing a clutch of talented youngsters who, by 1951–52, were beginning to come good. All they needed, it seemed, was an experienced head to fire them on the field. In Charlie Mitten, they found the perfect foil for their youthful talents. But it was to prove not enough.

The Craven Cottagers were already on that seemingly self-perpetuating downward spiral that every struggling club on the slide is familiar with when the Bogotá Bandit first stepped out in the white shirt and black shorts of his new club. Signing the soccer outlaw was clearly a last desperate throw of the dice by a board which at least was more concerned with whether he could play football than with his rebel tendencies.

Fulham hadn't had a win for 17 weeks when the Mitten bombshell first exploded at Craven Cottage. A visiting Middlesbrough side were demolished by an electrifying display of wing-raiding that saw the home side hit six goals without reply – it could have been ten, enthused a rapturous press. The *Sunday Pictorial* said Mitten had been the 'general who inspired the rout. It was not so much that Middlesbrough were a poor side, but the fact that Fulham seemed transformed by the ex-Bogotá boy.'

Mitten blasted in two of the goals in between supplying a flow of 'pinpoint passes that gave his colleagues chances in turn'. Cheeky Charlie was on his way to writing himself into the folklore of yet another football club. The headlines even forecast that 'Mitten could make Fulham safe'. But, in truth, that task was beyond the skills of even Charlie Mitten. What he did do over the next three seasons of Second Division football was to inspire the Fulham forward line into becoming one of the most formidable attacking formations in the league. With players like Arthur Stevens, Bobby Robson, Bedford Jezzard and Johnny Haynes, recalled Mitten, how could he have done otherwise?

'At Fulham, we had an almost-good side – and a very talented forward line. I was 31, the senior man, and at the top of my powers, in my prime. I'd been around, and we had team chats, but I wasn't treated as a star, nor did I want to be. In football, you don't need players coming to you to tell you you're good. They have a respect for you based on what you've done and they see it for themselves on the field. But one man doesn't make a team.

'They had these terrific young players – like Robson and Haynes, neither of whom had been capped then – who were just coming through. But it wasn't quite enough. All good players must have other good footballers to play with. When I look back on the teams I've managed and played for, I come to the conclusion that a team needs a squad of seven or eight top-quality players to be a great side. If we'd had that at Fulham, we'd have done something.'

That's being unduly self-deprecating, as anyone who watched Fulham during those days would tell you. The fans flocked to watch the Craven Cottage forward line take apart some of the best defences in the country – and groaned as their own side leaked the goals that, match after match, denied Fulham the full fruits of victory. But it was entertaining to watch – a veritable goal-feast every game.

'We had the makings of a good side. Our forward lines could certainly score goals, 70 or 80 a season. The trouble was, our defence would give away 90 or 100. At the back, we had some fine players like Jim Taylor, Joe Bacuzzi and Eddie

Lowe, but we needed maybe one or two more top-class defenders. There was one match in which we beat Chelsea 6–4. It was good for the spectators; it certainly put bums on seats at Fulham and kept the chairman [showbiz comic legend Tommy Trinder] smiling – but didn't do our goal average much good!'

But having good reason to smile were the young inside trio of that forward line, Bedford Jezzard, Johnny Haynes and Bobby Robson, who all went on to win England international honours – and more. Haynes was to win 56 caps and Robson 20 – as well as the bed-of-nails national team managership. Before his death, Johnny Haynes, one of the all-time England greats, recalled his feelings about his first match alongside Mitten. 'As a 13 year old, I'd seen Charlie at Wembley in the 1948 final against Blackpool and there I was, four years later, playing with him on the left-wing – I couldn't believe it. He was my first left-wing partner in the Fulham first team, and I've got very fond memories of him. He was an electrifying player with a great left foot. I'm sure he would have got more caps if he hadn't stepped out of line.'

But the crucial thing, Charlie pointed out, was that Fulham had two wingmen who could deliver for the frontmen. 'They were always pleased to put them away – especially Bobby. He was a good player, along with Haynes, Jezzard and Stevens. Arthur was a natural outside-right who could cross the ball from the wing, straight to a man, no bother, every time. It's a skill that's been lost today.'

The joker in the pack among the Craven Cottage comedians was Bedford Jezzard, who was always in for a jape on or off the park. Unfortunately, injury cut short a promising career which could have included further England honours. Jezzard was an old-style bustling, deep-lying forward with the pace and heading ability to be a deadly finisher in and around the six-yard box. He was later team manager at Craven Cottage. 'Charlie was quite a character,' recalled Jezzard, who died in May 2005, 'and he had a good time with us even though it was towards the end of his career. In the first game he played for us, he scored a superb goal, and that set him off. We had quite a forward line after Charlie arrived. He was a very talented, skilled player, and very confident – he used to gee us up and tell us we could do it with the best. We'd score 80 to 100 goals a season and played some incredibly entertaining football.'

There was no doubting who was the inspiration of the Craven Cottage attack. Assessing Fulham's record in the 1954 promotion stakes, the *Soccer Sun* reported:

> The arch-strategist of this line-up is undoubtedly Charlie Mitten, aggravatingly clever ball artist, but oh so very good to watch. Add to this his ability to cross the ball perfectly (no other winger compares with him) a lethal shot and his expert penalty-taking, and you have just about the complete winger. The power of Fulham's forward line would have taken the London side back into the First Division if their prowess had been matched by a better defence. Mitten, Haynes, Jezzard, Robson and Stevens are as lethal as any attack in the country.

Bobby Robson, lately of Newcastle United, Barcelona and Portuguese sides Sporting Lisbon and Porto, can still recall the effect Cheeky Charlie's arrival had both on the field and in the dressing-room. 'Fantastic – Charlie was a marvellous player. We knew he was one of the Bogotá outlaws and that United had refused to take him back. So we got him, and he became our old maestro. He had a wonderful left foot, but the great thing about Charlie was his ultra-confidence. He had a great temperament, so cool that you always thought you were going to be match-winners.'

If there was one single player who impressed Charlie, it was

Johnny Haynes, who became a cultured playmaker and also a master of precision passing. Haynes was certainly a precocious talent, and he found it difficult to conceal his exasperation at the on-field shortcomings of lesser mortals. It earned him a reputation for being arrogant, which was unfortunate and not warranted.

'I played alongside Johnny Haynes for three years and it was obvious that he was going to be a fine player. It was just a question of time as he developed. It was true that he was a bit of a hothead in his early days but that was because he had an intense love of the game. He was a perfectionist and was inclined to give the impression that he was big-headed on the field. Onlookers often went away thinking that Haynes was a "naughty boy", and it was true that he was rather outspoken in the dressing-room. But if there was any criticism at all, it wouldn't be from me. As far as I was concerned, if we needed a goal and I'd gone down the wing and plonked it on Johnny's or Bedford's head and they scored, well, they were entitled to feel top dog, weren't they? If I put a nice one on Johnny's head, I'd say, "Well done, John. A good header, son!" And he'd reply laconically, "A perfect cross, Charles. Couldn't have done it if it hadn't been crossed right." But Johnny, like many youngsters before him, learned his lesson in time, and he turned out to be a very successful England player.'

Fulham always seemed to finish up also-rans, despite the talent in the team. By the time the club had succeeded in getting back into the top flight in 1958, Charlie Mitten was long gone. But Fulham were never dull: they were a team of entertainers – just like many of the fans who turned up to watch. Charlie recalled Fulham as the 'showbiz club' that visiting celebrities would come and watch.

'You'd often see top variety stars from America or the Continent on Saturday afternoons sitting in the box at Craven Cottage with Tommy Trinder, our chairman. I remember him coming into the dressing-room before a game and saying,

"Right, you lucky people, whoever scores the first goal gets my overcoat!" It was a big, expensive Crombie. I never did win it – and I can't recall anyone else getting it either.'

Among the regular visitors to Craven Cottage were FA secretary Sir Stanley Rous and England manager Walter Winterbottom, who, of course, went on to cap three of Fulham's scintillating forward line – Haynes and Jezzard as well as Robson after he'd moved to West Bromwich Albion. But despite the devastating displays of Mitten's wing-play, there was no room for a Bogotá Bandit in the England team.

'I met Sir Stanley and talked to him quite often – he used to come down to Fulham to watch the matches, and we'd talk after the game. He was a decent, down-to-earth chap and seemed to be on the players' side, but for the sake of his job, he kept quiet. He told me plainly that I couldn't be selected for England because "discipline comes first". But of course they had a lot of good players to pick from at the time. They had Tom Finney. He was a top-class player, although not a natural left-winger. They excluded me, but there was always someone else around the corner.'

That Fulham didn't do as well as they might, Mitten felt, was down to something more than an ordinary defence. The dressing-room seemed to lack that unity of purpose and spirit of camaraderie that had propelled Manchester United. Most of the tension, he recalled, arose out of the dual system of management he found in place when he arrived at Craven Cottage. Bill Dodgin was nominally in charge, with responsibility for team selection, but there was also a general manager, Frank Osborne. There was the feeling among the players that their team manager was not fully in control and that important decisions were often made elsewhere.

'Dodgin's job was very difficult under these circumstances. If the team were doing well, he would probably have his say in selections; if we were doing badly, it was taken entirely out of his hands. I was always very much against this system of a team manager with limited powers; it is fraught with danger. It is the short way to football suicide.

'A manager who is worthy of the title should have his finger on the pulse of the club. He should be conversant with all the club's business, whether it be the signing of an amateur player on professional forms or the buying of a senior player for a seven-figure transfer fee. A manager worthy of the name must have a grasp of the financial side of his club and consider items as if they were his own business. And a club looking for a so-called team manager with limited powers is looking for a stooge. It can never work out – and the facts prove that it doesn't.

'There's no doubt I was at times very outspoken at Fulham. But I used to feel very sorry about it afterwards, because I knew that I had hurt some player's feelings. I certainly had a barney or two with Frank Osborne, but it was only because I didn't like the set-up. It resulted in two camps, two separate factions tugging against each other, and that was wrong. Fulham should have been one of the most successful clubs in London. Craven Cottage had a lot of talent, a wonderful following, and Tommy Trinder was popular with the players. Our team was always more than three-quarters of a loaf, but never quite a full one.'

But whatever else Mitten did at Fulham, he never gave less than 100 per cent on a Saturday afternoon. The proof, if it were needed, was that while he was treated as an outcast by the national FA, the London region FA had absolutely no qualms about calling him up for representative games, including several foreign trips. It was during one of these matches – against a West German XI – that floodlighting was first used at Wembley. (Floodlights had been tried in friendlies by several clubs before being given the official seal of approval in the FA Cup second-round replay between Carlisle and Darlington at Newcastle on 28 November 1955.)

'The officials of the London FA were the best

administrators I met in soccer. Their human approach brought out the best in the players, and we never lost a game against some of the best representative sides in Europe – because we always pulled out that little bit extra. It was our way of repaying the officials who extended the hand of friendship. Charles Fuller, secretary of the London FA, was particularly well liked. I look back on these games as my most enjoyable honours in football. There was a lot of speculation in the press and talk on the soccer grapevine that I would get another chance in the international side. But the Bogotá episode had blotted my copybook with the hierarchy, and once that happened, you were sunk.'

None are so blind as those who don't want to see. In October 1953, Sir Stanley Rous had been at Craven Cottage when Fulham could manage only a 2–2 draw against a quick-tackling Stoke City. But he told Fulham's directors after the game: 'Charlie Mitten's display was the best by an outside-left I've seen this season.' It made no difference. Rous, although one of the ablest and most forward-looking administrators the game has had (he introduced red and yellow cards), was a prisoner of the entrenched old guard. George Harley wrote in the *Daily Mail*: 'Charlie Mitten, one of the Bogotá bad boys, paid the full penalty for that indiscretion. The selectors may find that they can ill afford to permit prejudice to deprive the England team of Mitten's striking combination of speed, craft and shooting power. At Fulham, Mitten and young Johnny Haynes have proved that they form the best left-wing in the country.'

Charlie would have added the name of Fulham left-half Eddie Lowe to make a left-side triangle he believed was unequalled in the league at that time.

The following week (10 October) at Ninian Park, Cardiff, England ran out 4–1 winners against a Wales side for whom full-back Alf Sherwood was a passenger on the wing for most of the game, after being concussed in an early collision. Then came the last warning, again studiously ignored.

It was the FA's 90th birthday celebrations against the Rest of Europe. Hungary, the Olympic champions, had withdrawn all their players, but the prevailing wisdom was that with or without the Hungarians, 'the Rest' had no chance. England struggled to a 4–4 draw with a last-minute, face-saving penalty – from an ice-cool Alf Ramsey – after trailing 3–1 for much of the game. That England got away with it was due in no small part to some timely wizardry from Stanley Matthews, recalled at 38. For the Rest, the Europeans showed they were streets ahead of England in technique and tactics.

But there was to be no comeback call to the colours for Mitten or, indeed, for Neil Franklin. Four weeks later, England ran into the hurricane from Hungary.

Despite the humiliation, the introverted English game stumbled in and out of three World Cup campaigns before the players' contract revolution and Alf Ramsey's equally revolutionary managerial appointment. But if there was to be a brief flowering of hope for the English game as players won their freedom, then 1966 was to prove a pyrrhic victory, thought Charlie Mitten. For in conquering the world against all the odds, the seeds were sown for the stagnation of English soccer for almost a generation, for reasons we shall discuss later.

At Fulham, 34-year-old Charlie Mitten was turning it on week after week. Matthews, at 42, was still doing it at [almost] every other international. (In May 1956, the Wizard of Dribble gave Nílton Santos, the best full-back in the world, the runaround in England's famous 4–2 win over Brazil at Wembley. Sir Stan recalled: 'Charlie was still a very good player while at Fulham – and a very nice man: cheeky. What I remember about Charlie was his greyhounds – I don't know how true it is, but they say he used to take his dogs down to the ground and the trainer used to massage them for him. That was Charlie! Ask him about the greyhounds!')

But Charlie knew there'd be no more honours for him.

Fulham always seemed to be not quite good enough in either the League or cup, and England weren't going to pick him again. 'I remember on one occasion, one of these selectors saying to me, "I tried to get you in, lad, but I was overruled." He might have been conning me, trying to fanny me up. There was nothing club directors liked better than talking to international players. It made them feel good.'

But if England were refusing to select him, Charlie himself was often in disagreement at the way the line-up was being picked at Craven Cottage. And he was beginning to think it was time that he was choosing his own team.

The opportunity came in a railway-carriage buffet-car and was to lead to the ground of the twisted spire in the heart of England where, in the deep midwinter, the master was tested again and found wanting.

# 13

# The Master Who Missed

The club's directors have slipped up – they ought to have signed this magician months ago. Call him Merlin Mitten from now on!

*Mansfield Chronicle Advertiser*

FROM THE MOMENT HE'D FIRST STEPPED OUT FOR THE FIRST team at Manchester United at the age of 25, through 12 months of combat on the far-flung, lush, dusty and jungle-green swards of Colombia, and back in England through four seasons at Craven Cottage, Charlie Mitten had never for a second doubted he had the skill and speed to beat any defender in the world. But in 1955, the whistle finally blew full-time for the left-winger. It's a moment which comes to every player, star or journeyman, but one which many choose to ignore. Charlie didn't.

'If you're taught correctly at 18 and 19, you'll be good at 25 and even better when you're 30 and over. It never leaves you; it just gets better all the time. The best full-back in the world is just an obstacle. Matt Busby would say to me, "Watch yourself, lad, this full-back is a bit rough." I'd say to my inner self, "No danger, boss, I can take care of him." When I went to South America, I felt I could take on anyone. If you know what you're going to do, you can do it without thinking. It's all in your head. What's not all in your head is pace.'

It happened overnight, just like that, and Charlie Mitten knew he'd never play at the highest level again. At 35 years old and in what was to prove his final season at Fulham, Charlie knew it was all over. He always remembered the exact moment. 'I woke up one morning and it wasn't there any more. My pace had gone. Yet, in myself, I'd never felt so good playing as when I was 35. I felt at my peak. The only thing that went from my game was that turn of speed. I got up one morning, went for a training run, and it wasn't there. And that was it.'

Charlie knew it was the end of the road at Craven Cottage when he found out that the club were looking around for another outside-left. Of course, he'd been half-expecting it and was philosophical enough to accept that it was time to move on, but the call had come rather sooner than he'd anticipated. No player finds it easy to accept that it's time to quit the fray. Why not play a few more months, one last season? Charlie decided to go immediately.

Then, by chance, he found his first manager's job. He'd been playing regularly in exhibition games for the All-Stars XI managed by Bob Jackson, which included greats like Stan Matthews. Indeed, it was because of these games that Charlie actually got to partner his idol and to learn at first hand how the maestro worked.

'It was in a match in Ireland, and I was playing inside-right to Stan. Being left-footed, of course, it was easy for me to play the ball to him. Stan said to me, "Give me the ball, Charlie, and I'll meet you up in the penalty area." I said, "OK, Stan," and I scored two goals. I realised then how Jimmy Mudie, Stan's partner at Blackpool, must have felt – giving Stan the passes and then collecting the goals at the other end! A good inside-man was what made brilliant one-off players like Matthews.'

It was on the train journey home from one of these matches that the opportunity at Mansfield Town came up. Charlie was discussing with Peter Docherty the pros and cons of moving from Fulham into a player–manager's job. Docherty advised that it was a good halfway house into management. He also mentioned the player–manager's job was vacant at Mansfield, that he knew the club's vice-chairman, Jack Taylor, quite well and that he would, if Charlie liked, put in a word for him.

It took the club a month to respond to Charlie's letter of application with an invitation to attend an interview. He recalled his feelings of utter gloom on the way to the club's Field Mill ground, wondering whether he was doing the right thing. 'What a dismal place Mansfield is in mid-February – it was bleak, dreary and at first I couldn't find anybody about. Then I stumbled into Syd Carter, the trainer, who'd also been filling the gap as manager after Freddie Steele had left. He made me feel very much at home and took me to his house for tea. Mansfield turned out to be the happiest club I've ever been at.'

Mitten's interview with the club's directors was pretty much a formality: the pedigree of the man applying for the job was hardly in question and terms were soon agreed. Charlie recalled his impression of the day he signed up to cross the player–manager divide.

'The Mansfield directors were all businessmen in the town – pretty much as in most other clubs at the time – usually well versed in the ways of business and with soccer very much a hobby. There seems to be something in-bred in these men who put their time and money into the game. It's as if football is a magic word to them. They like to drive up in their cars on a Saturday and enjoy the preferential treatment that goes with a football directorship. I suspect the most pleasurable moment in most football directors' lives is the natter over a drink in the boardroom after the match with the directors of the opposing club. These men get untold satisfaction from feeling they're on the inside of football, even though they'll never ever know what it's like out there in the middle actually doing it.'

On Friday, 3 February 1956, Charlie Mitten was transferred from glamorous Fulham to entirely unfashionable Mansfield Town. The next day, he made his debut as player–manager in the game against Wrexham. Mansfield paid £3,500 for him – quite a sizeable fee for the Stags in those days. Charlie had made 160 league and cup appearances for Fulham, scoring 33 goals – and left a proud London club with many beautiful memories.

Charlie saw the move to Mansfield as an even bigger gamble than the flight to Bogotá. The Stags were a struggling club hovering near the foot of the Third Division North, with home gates averaging around 3,500. But it was a risk which Mitten fearlessly took. He believed totally in himself, that he had something to offer, and that here was a challenge which would progress his knowledge and career in the beautiful game. But perhaps most importantly of all, he was impressed by the boardroom approach. Vice-chairman Jack Taylor, a man he took an immediate liking to, told him there'd be no money for anything – but he promised Charlie that he would be allowed to get on with the job without interference.

'I looked at the Mansfield job in this way: my days at Fulham were numbered, so why not move to a smaller club in the lower class of football where I could be of some use as a player, and also at the same time serve my own apprenticeship in football management? If I could make Mansfield pay its way, I thought to myself, then I would be successful anywhere in soccer. It was a hard task from the start. There was no youth scheme, no scouting, practically nothing in the way of organisation. It was a desolate, run-down set-up with hardly a decent player on the books. Mansfield's basic problem was the same as many Third and Fourth Division sides. With gates of £400 a fortnight, they were having to meet a wage bill of £500 a week. I was in trouble from the outset. But if I could put that right by enticing bigger gates, by putting a better side on the field, then I'd consider that I had passed through my managerial apprenticeship.'

But first there was Charlie Mitten's second and last red card – and it came within a fortnight of him pulling on a Mansfield Town jersey. In his first game, Town had hammered Wrexham 6–1 (although Charlie didn't get on the score sheet). The following week, the Stags were playing Darlington and Charlie recalled he had called up Oscar Fox, a brilliant young player, at right-half. But when Fox was injured in a clash with Darlington's Dickie Davies, Mitten remonstrated with the Darlington player and an altercation ensued which led to Mitten being dismissed by the referee. Charlie never forgot the incident, which he deeply regretted.

'It happened just as they reported it. I was incensed that an older player – someone I'd actually played with before – should take it out on a kid. The lad was too good for him and was beating him, so he'd been kicking Fox and injured him. I lost my temper, and I said to Davies when I cracked him one, "It's an old pro that's giving you one back now, Dickie! You shouldn't be doing that. You should be above it." The referee heard this, and he said to me, "I'm very sorry, Charles, you'll have to go off." Davies never said a word. He hadn't dared to try and kick me; he knew he'd get one back. He'd picked on a young kid who was green and taken advantage of him.'

Charlie's long-held belief was that part of the problem in stamping out this sort of behaviour and giving skilful players protection is not that referees are too lenient but that they haven't the experience. Most, not having played the game, can't always spot the calculated, cynical and deliberate foul. They do their best to administer the law according to the rules, but they haven't the know-how, for example, to spot the heinous crime of the 'over-the-ball' tackle which can instantly snap a player's leg. Charlie was uncompromisingly fierce on this question.

'It's the worst foul in football, and too many referees think it's a legitimate tackle. They just do not know. That's why I think the best referees would be ex-players who come into the game at 35, after having the playing experience. That's so important because referees aren't seeing it, and players are getting away with dirty play time after time. It's the same with tackling from behind – going straight through the man. It's so obviously a deliberate foul. That's the same as going over the top, and it's almost as dangerous. It's a deliberate foul and they should be off. There should be no yellow card first – any deliberate foul should get the red card instantly. There should be no warning about their play – they should be off the field. They should go. Of course it would help skilful players. It would encourage all players to play skilfully instead of dirtily.'

Charlie's out-of-character transgression at Wrexham is far outweighed by what he achieved at Mansfield. The record speaks for itself; and, on the way, there were moments of magic, mirth and shocked amazement. By the time of the Easter programme, just eight weeks after Mitten had taken over, the *Mansfield Chronicle Advertiser* was recording a stunning transformation: Town had taken twelve points from a possible sixteen, scored twenty-seven goals and conceded six – only one at Field Mill. 'That's Town's record since Charlie Mitten walked in with something akin to magic. The club's directors have slipped up – they ought to have signed this magician months ago. Call him Merlin Mitten from now on! Depression has vanished from Town's headquarters since he took over.'

The secret of that magic was very simple: Charlie Mitten committed his team to a policy which, basically, amounted to attack or die – and he picked players who were willing and able to put it into effect. No one believed a club like Mansfield could risk such a strategy. Joe Eaton, a pre-Mitten Mansfield reserves player, and later the league's longest-serving club secretary, recalled the electrifying effect the switch had on the

Stags' fortunes. 'Charlie Mitten was one of those rare managers who believed in all-out attack, because he believed that was the way the game should be played. We'd be getting matches with plenty of goals – results like 4–2 and 5–3. Although we conceded a few, we scored a lot, and it was terrific. You could see Charlie had been with Manchester United – their delightful attacking football rubbed off on our forwards, and the fans loved it.'

Fans old *and* new. Gates soared and exceeded 10,000 for the first time in more than five years with the Easter fixtures in that first Mitten season. Local derby games against Chesterfield, Lincoln and Notts County attracted crowds of up to 14,000. And there was never any doubting who was the star of the show. Joe Eaton said: 'Charlie just loved playing – you couldn't stop him. He turned out for most of our matches while he was here – he only left himself out if he was injured. He was a real favourite: he had an absolutely beautiful left foot, and he was still doing tricks down the wing at 36. He had one where he would somehow trap a high ball with his backside; the crowds loved it. He was a very, very skilful player. He would surely have been in the England side if he hadn't gone to Bogotá. He and Franklin were frozen out. Someone with Charlie's reputation coming to the club was wonderful, quite a sensation.'

The big – and pleasant – surprise, Charlie recalled, was the backing he got from the supporters club. Their amazing fund-raising efforts helped him finance some astute purchases on the transfer market. Charlie persuaded the homesick Busby Babe Sammy Chapman, who had gone back to Ireland, to return on a free transfer from Crusaders and later sold him to Portsmouth for £7,000. He signed Jimmy Glazzard from Everton on a free transfer, three months after the Merseysiders had bought him for £3,750. Barry Thomas came from Leicester for £4,000 and was sold for £15,000 two seasons later to Scunthorpe, then in the Second Division.

Dennis Uphill was bought in from Coventry City for a mere £1,250. The result was that in his first full season there was £12,500 surplus on the transfer account, and Charlie was able to spend money on ground improvements – expenditure almost unheard of for most clubs at that level, but which Charlie believed was crucial in encouraging new supporters and fostering old loyalties.

'Mansfield was the best job I ever had. They had a top-class chairman and a board of local people who were prepared to let me manage. But because I hadn't any money to buy players, I had to keep my eye open for footballers who couldn't get in their first team and who might be available on a free transfer – like Lindy Delapenha. A brilliant outside-right, he was the first black player at Mansfield. I signed him from Middlesbrough the same month I left Mansfield to go to Newcastle. He was in his 30s and Boro thought he was past it. Stan Matthews changed that view a bit.' (Jamaican-born Lloyd Lindbergh Delapenha was an amateur at Arsenal before moving to Portsmouth in 1948 and then Middlesborough. In eight seasons in the North-East, he hit 90 goals, a better wing strike rate than even Charlie Mitten.)

A youth policy was instituted and promising local youngsters given their head in the first team as soon as they were good enough, irrespective of their age. The *Mansfield Chronicle Advertiser* recorded how it started six weeks after Mitten had arrived: 'This evening from five o'clock onwards, some of the 800 applicants will be on view at Field Mill – the gates open to the public – with trials for about 50 of the 16 and 17 year olds. The youth policy is under way. Like all shrewd managers, Charlie Mitten has an eye on the future.'

These youngsters included Mitten's own son John, who was also a talented cricketer and on the Nottinghamshire county ground staff. A left-winger like his dad, John made the Mansfield first team before Charlie was lured away from Field Mill to his biggest challenge in management at Newcastle. In his first full season as manager, Mansfield Town finished sixth from the top of the Third Division North. And all the youngsters who came through the youth policy were playing reserves soccer in the London Combination, many challenging for a first-team place. They would certainly have earned it. As Joe Eaton recalled: 'The standard was really a bit too much for us. We were playing the reserve sides from clubs like Chelsea, Spurs and Arsenal. On one visit to Field Mill, Spurs' reserves included four current internationals and a young Bobby Smith having a try-out.'

Charlie's strategy relied on blending the old with the new, the skilful with the less subtle: 'I got a lad called Fred Morris from Walsall for nothing. When I asked around, "What's this lad Morris like?" I was told, "Well, Charlie, if petrol were brains, he wouldn't get out of the garage." Which was unfair. He was a big strong lad, as fast as a deer, who could run through a brick wall. I found he was far more intelligent than he'd been given credit for. In the Third Division, you needed more aggression, and you wouldn't worry too much how skilfully he went past a man, so long as he got past. It was Fred going like a bull down the right side, and me down the left. I used to do a few back-heels and tricks – it really excited the crowds.'

But it was in ball skills that Charlie put his faith for Mansfield's future, training in his tracksuit with the younger players.

'We were always working out some nice moves, like we did at United. It was easy with these boys because no one had got hold of them before to teach them these skills. This is what football's all about – players always like to play with the ball, and you'll find that they'll run a mile for you with the ball at their feet, where they wouldn't run 100 yards without one. It just shows that if you can see potential, what a player's got, and it suits your team plans, you can polish them and bring them on. And if you can't polish them, you get rid of the player. You tell them straight: "You're not good enough." It's hard, but it's the right thing to do. Because if you can't play football, why the hell are you trying to do it for a living?'

One boy given his chance was Mitten's son John. As well as making the first team at outside-left, John was called up for England youth duty. He was in the team that played Holland in Amsterdam in which a young West Ham player made his international debut: one R. Moore. Another youngster who seized his chance was a wing-half called Syd Watson, who went on to become a first-team regular after Charlie had left Town. Watson was arguably one of the few people in Mansfield who was glad to see the back of Charlie – so he'd get more of the ball during a game.

Joe Eaton said: 'After a game, Syd would complain he was always under orders from Charlie to give him the ball. But Charlie would always know what to do with it. He had a terrific burst of speed over 20 yards, and once he got the ball, that's all he needed. We were a small club with no money and fair-to-average players and one or two older heads like Charlie. But he made do all right. His attacking football went down very well with the board and the fans, and we moved up the table. That's when Newcastle got him. They'd obviously seen what he'd done for Mansfield.'

One feat above all others has become part of Mansfield Town folklore – and one of the rare episodes in his career that Charlie Mitten didn't relish recalling. It was the extraordinary match in which he missed a penalty-kick, not once, but twice! It happened in the game against Chesterfield – town of the church of the twisted spire – at the Derbyshire club's Recreation Ground on Christmas Day 1956, in the days when games were played on both 25 and 26 December.

'We got a penalty and, of course, Charlie took it,' recalled Joe Eaton. 'He shot and hit the goalkeeper's legs. The ball came back out and Charlie shot again, but it hit the post and came out, and we ended up losing 1–0. It was a local derby and there were over 12,000 there, one of the biggest gates we've ever had for a Christmas derby. The press noted that it really was an occasion for Charlie Mitten to miss from the penalty spot. It was quite a sensation. They were talking about it for weeks after. It was an eleven o'clock kick-off, and his mind must have been on the turkey.'

Despite committing the unforgivable sin, Charlie had no regrets about his detour through the Third Division. 'In the end, I like to think Mansfield finished up with a very good side, and I ended up with the managerial experience I needed. I was happy that I was able to help such a grand little club so much in my two and a half years with them.'

Lifelong Mansfield supporter Jack Retter, official Town contributor to the PFA Factfile who compiled a history of the club for its 1997 centenary, said Mitten's contribution as a player was 'outstanding', especially for someone of his age. In two and a half years at Mansfield, he recalled, Charlie was rarely injured and missed only nine games – three of them so his son John could play at outside-left and three others to allow another youngster, Bobby Anderson, to have a run-out. He made 100 appearances, scoring 25 goals. 'It would be a pretty good scoring rate for a striker – and a young one – never mind a winger. His playing record was quite remarkable for a man of 36 – he certainly looked after himself. And as a manager, considering what he had to work with, Charlie did quite a good job really in very difficult financial circumstances.'

That managerial experience was to be tested to the limit when Charlie Mitten, football outlaw, found himself poacher-turned-gamekeeper. He was caught in the crossfire of an embattled boardroom that attempted to sabotage his own soccer revolution, while sparking another that was to change the face of football forever.

# 14

# Power Games

> If you put 11 black-and-white dogs on the field [at
> Newcastle], you'd get 30,000 coming to watch.
>
> Matt Busby, 1958

**OF ALL THE MEMORIES OF THREE TURBULENT YEARS AS** manager of Newcastle United, the ones Charlie Mitten always found most amusing were the tales of dogs. First there was Matt Busby's caustic commentary on the state of play at St James' Park. Then there was the matter of his 'hotline' to the dogs, which was one of the hottest in a litany of newspaper stories Cheeky Charlie generated during his stewardship. The latter tale was always vehemently denied by Charlie. Not that he wasn't a keen follower of greyhound racing, which he was. Or that he hadn't owned several dogs himself, which he had. What amazed him was the sheer inventiveness of the story, telling of how Newcastle had gone to the dogs – literally as well as metaphorically.

Mitten made no secret of his fondness for greyhounds, and he had regularly brought the dogs to be seen by club players at Old Trafford and Craven Cottage. Johnny Haynes recalled: 'It was the funniest thing I ever remember about Charlie at

Fulham. I took a bit of a knock one Saturday and went down to Craven Cottage for treatment. I went into the treatment room – and there on the physio's table is one of Charlie's greyhounds getting attention from the trainer. One of his dogs was injured, and he was trying to get it fit for a race meeting – and I couldn't get on the table for this dog!'

Charlie refused to deny such shaggy dog tales: 'It's perfectly true – unlike a lot of the Newcastle stories. At Fulham, I did have a dog which I used to race at Stamford Bridge track. I brought it in to the Cottage for treatment. There's no better way than the dog on the table and the physio doing his stuff. I did the same at United with my dogs there. If they got injured or pulled a muscle, I would come back to old Trafford in the afternoon and get Tom Curry to give them the sonic treatment on the physio's table. During the winter, I used to stand with the dogs stark naked and we'd all get the sun-ray treatment. It certainly toned your muscles up.'

Charlie Mitten's lifelong love affair with greyhound racing is a matter of record. He owned several dogs during his career. It began at Manchester, continued in London during his years at Fulham and his enthusiasm was undiminished when he came to Newcastle. John Gibson, now executive sports editor of the *Newcastle Evening Chronicle*, was a teenage fan at St James' Park when Mitten first exploded on to Tyneside, and he's never forgotten the impression Charlie made. 'It was an amazingly colourful time in Newcastle's history. We had emerged from a very successful period of having won the FA cup three times during the 1950s when Charlie came in – straight into the ongoing boardroom war. The club was full of wars in those days. It was a hell of a time. We had the Eastham case as well as the tales, true or false, which went around at the time, of Charlie's blower system for bets in his manager's office. And of him training his dog – it's gone down in local folklore how Charlie is supposed to have thrown Len White off the treatment table at St James' Park so he could have his dog's hind leg treated by the physio because it was running at Brough Park that night.'

Given the internecine boardroom warfare which characterised his tenure at St James' Park, it is inconceivable that Mitten could have survived as long as he did if there had been any element of misconduct on his part as manager. At any one time, throughout his stormy three years in the North-East, half the board would have happily fired him instantly on the slightest pretext. Success or failure on the football pitch didn't come into it; this was small-town politics with a vengeance. The miracle was that Charlie survived so long and achieved so much in such a bear's den. Kevin Keegan had a lot to be grateful for. The remarkable revival of Newcastle United shows what can be done at a football club where a boardroom is working in harmony with a charismatic, energetic and enterprising manager. (But, as Sir Bobby Robson found out, at Newcastle they really do believe the buck stops with the manager, no matter how big the name. And now Graham Souness is in the hottest seat in football.)

In 1958, when Charlie applied for the job described by soccer pundits at the time as football's 'hottest hot seat', he had decided to quit Mansfield over a difference of opinion. He wanted to hang up his boots at 37 and concentrate full-time on building up the club and on his ambitious plans for Division Two status. But the board prevaricated, ironically because they felt his playing talents were too valuable as a crowd-puller at Field Mill. Charlie agreed to play on for one more season in return for a full management contract, but was unable to get such a commitment. For a man whose approach had been as direct off the field as on, this was too much.

'I had told my directors I would only be prepared to play another season, and then I'd like to concentrate on the management side. It was not that I was feeling tired or past playing, but I believed that by packing up as a player I would have more time to concentrate on scouting duties and the things that go to make up a manager's job. At a meeting with the Mansfield directors in June 1958, I again asked for a proper manager's contract when I'd finished playing in 12 months' time. I had never pressed this point with the directors before, and I was quite surprised and rather hurt when they were evasive about the whole matter. They obviously thought I was too useful to them as a player.

'My argument was that I had established myself at Mansfield. We had finished sixth in the Third Division North in the vital season which saw the two sections of the Third Division split up to form the new Third and Fourth Divisions. I had brought a higher standard of football to Mansfield than had ever been there before, and, in that period, the club coffers had been boosted by something near to £12,000 by incoming transfer fees. Yet I was constantly told that only a "full board meeting" could decide. I was absolutely disgusted with the whole thing. Such is the kind of treatment often meted out to managers by gentlemen, businessmen, who become directors of a professional football club – although I found chairman Jack Taylor and vice-chairman Colonel W. Mein straight in dealing with me.'

An uncharacteristically depressed Charlie Mitten decided that his talents might be better appreciated elsewhere, and he told his wife he was going to apply for another job. As it happened, there were two managerial vacancies at the time in the First Division, Blackpool and Newcastle, and Charlie applied for both. Blackpool, seeking a successor to Joe Smith, put him on the shortlist, along with Ron Stuart, who was then boss at Scunthorpe, and Walter Galbraith of Accrington Stanley. But Charlie was unable to keep an interview appointment at Bloomfield Road – and Blackpool, rather than wait, appointed Ron Stuart.

As for the Newcastle job, Charlie always insisted he'd never received acknowledgement of his application. (He subsequently found out it was because club secretary Ted Hall had been absent because of illness at the time.) So a phone call one evening from United chairman Alderman William McKeag, inviting him to an interview next day at St James' Park, came as a complete surprise. Two other candidates for the job were Les Goulden, the England international inside-forward and former manager at Watford, and Eddie Lever, then managing Portsmouth, who blazed a post-war trail in the First Division but had fallen on hard times (Pompey were relegated in 1959).

It was common knowledge at the time that Newcastle, a once-great club with a proud tradition, were also on the slide. After winning promotion to the First Division in 1948, the Magpies became a force to be reckoned with, rarely out of the top half of the table and winning the FA Cup in 1951, 1952 and 1955. But in 1957 they finished sixth off the bottom and the following season dropped to fourth. The team's remorseless slide was due to the fact that the club had become a house divided. As the *Daily Express* put it: 'Newcastle was better known for its boardroom battles than its prowess on the field. The managership was a job that might have scared the pants off more experienced men.' But Cheeky Charlie had never ducked a challenge in his life, and he decided to go for broke. He knew his football and felt confident that he could transform the situation at Newcastle, so long as the boardroom kept out of the dressing-room.

'I was the first of three applicants to be interviewed and had about half an hour to talk with the gentlemen around the boardroom table. I didn't pull any punches at the interview. It's no good daintily buttering up matters if you intend changing things when you get the job. You must start the way you mean to continue. I told the Newcastle directors the way I had gone on at Mansfield and said that I would want full control of team selection, scouting, training, and buying and selling of players. I would submit items to the board so they could talk it over and tie up the financial ends – which, of course, is their directive job. If they were employing me as their football expert, I wanted all the reins, as far as the football side of the club went, in my hands. If I was going to "hang" eventually, as many soccer managers had done before, I wanted it to be in my own hands.'

Charlie admitted he knew perfectly well that there was boardroom faction-fighting at Newcastle; how could he not have known – there are few secrets on the soccer grapevine. And, in any case, Newcastle had a habit of washing their dirty linen in public, in the newspapers. But he thought he could handle the real business of the football, while others played the political games. As he later admitted, he couldn't have been more wrong.

'I was well aware of the strife between McKeag and his co-director, Stan Seymour. I was also certain in my own mind what were the rights and wrongs of this matter. In football, there is quite a bit of freemasonry. People talk, players talk among themselves and there are very few secrets inside the game. This boardroom trouble had been going on for some time. I remembered years previously going to St James' Park when I was playing with Manchester United, and this directorial awkwardness was going on then. As manager at Mansfield, I had bought two players from Newcastle – Charlie Crowe and Stan Keery – so, of course, I was kept up to date on the gossip from Newcastle and had formed my own opinion about the whole matter.

'I gave it a lot of thought before I decided to move to the North-East. The way I reasoned was that if these directors gave me control and are decent people – that's the main thing, decency – and they let common sense prevail, then things are bound to come right. I must have a chance. Anyway, it's a challenge. If I make good, then I've got a good job; if I don't, then I've dropped a clanger. The one thing I believed in unswervingly was my own knowledge of the game. I moved to Newcastle because I had ambitions to be a top-class manager.'

These were the thoughts of Charlie Mitten when he was offered the job which was to put him off football management for life and see his hopes for a soccer revolution he'd harboured since 1950 implode. But before he took the plunge, he tried to assuage his own misgivings by seeking advice. And the one man qualified to give it, he knew, was his old boss at Manchester United.

'I'd gone up for the interview and stayed with Charlie Crowe. He'd remained based in the North-East and would come down for matches at Mansfield on Saturdays. I was in his house when the phone rang, and Newcastle told me that I'd got the job and that I was to come down to the ground to sign the contract. They would be prepared to offer me a one-year contract. I didn't want that. But they said we didn't know each other. I hadn't expected such a sudden decision, and I decided to have a word with Matt Busby on the phone. He said to me, "The good points are they're a club who could match Manchester United and they get good crowds – if you put 11 black-and-white dogs on the field, you'd get 30,000 coming to watch." I said, "That's what's tempting me." But Matt says, "On the other hand, you've got the power game among the directors." He knew all about that. He said, "They've got more managers than players. You'll have a problem, and I don't know whether you're big enough to get over them. It's no a job I would take, laddie. I don't think anyone could win up there." Looking back, the board saying they didn't know *me* was the lesser of two evils. *I* didn't know the board, and that proved to be the bigger evil. If *I* had known *them*, I'd never have signed.'

The *Daily Mail* reported without a hint of irony: 'The compensation for filling one of soccer's hottest seats is £3,000 a year, one of the best-paid jobs in football. So the former Manchester United outside-left who flew to Bogotá in search of soccer gold in 1950 has finally struck it rich.'

But it was clear that Charlie was going to earn his money.

According to the *Sunday Express*, Newcastle was 'a cockpit of trouble'. United had been swept out of the FA Cup by Third Division Scunthorpe, gates were slumping, and it was said the players hadn't even a single new football to train with, just 11 shabby leathers – and this at a club notorious for having lavished £400,000 on players since the war. 'It was a club torn by intrigue, suspicion and backroom bickering . . . disgruntled stars seldom knowing from week to week whether they were going to play.'

When Mitten took over at Newcastle at the age of 37, he was the youngest manager in the Football League, another record in his career. But there was an old head on those young shoulders. Within weeks, he'd sacked the existing scouting staff and appointed a new squad of talent-seekers to scout the North-East and Scotland. A new-style Continental strip was introduced, with a wide-band edging on the bottom of shorts – an idea copied from Dynamo Moscow – so players could glimpse each other easily without taking their eye off the ball. He began a review of playing staff, too, and, in the first season, set up a youth policy where before there was none. The gymnasium was being used as a tearoom, and the club didn't even have a medical room. There were no treatment lamps – no equipment at all, in fact, beyond the dressing-room table. A medical room was immediately installed under the stand, and qualified physios were appointed.

Charlie recalled his first 100 days: 'I had to be the jack of all trades at the time. We had three trainers, but they were nothing more than kit-men, bandage men, odd-jobbers – not really coaches, not even trainers. They couldn't conduct a proper training session of exercises with the players – they'd be doing sprints, jogs, running and laps with the players just hoping twelve o'clock would come up so that they could get the ball out. You should start straight away by putting a ball at their feet – you'll get more out of players than you'll ever get making them run laps. That's far too monotonous. They'll run because they've got to run, but it's under duress. It's soul destroying. Give them the ball and they'll run about all day. That's what they're going to have to do come Saturday, so they might as well take the ball with them as much as possible in weekly training. The number-one thing is mastery of the ball. I'd never like a player to turn to me and say, "I didn't get hold of the ball during the match, boss, because we don't practise enough with the ball." My regime included every player having a ball with him all the time and only leaving it – outside the door – when he went to the toilet.'

Mitten found that there was a good clutch of senior players – men like Alf McMichael, Dick Keith, Bobby Mitchell, Bob Stokoe, Jimmy Scoular, George Eastham and Lennie White. Many had international experience, but training discipline was lax, dressing-room morale low and personal animosities even spilled out onto the field.

'They were good players, yet the club was not doing well because there was so much bickering among the players as well as on the board. Scoular and Stokoe didn't get on. There was actually a fight on the field once. So I had to read them the riot act, and I told them if they wanted to fight, it had to be after the match, if at all. In fact, if there was any more of it, I didn't want either of them at the club. I told them straight, no messing, and that blaming each other for mistakes on the field was affecting the results. They settled down. It helped, of course, that I would go out training with the boys and never asked any player to do anything I couldn't show him. I was a tracksuit manager.'

Of course, given his pedigree, the players tried to persuade Charlie to turn out for the first team. But he stuck to his decision to quit the fray. Charlie knew the real hope of Newcastle lay in youth, and he set out to find, polish and bring on the young hopefuls.

'I was tempted. I thought I could have put myself on as outside-left – in training, I was putting the ball into the far corner of the net from the edge of the box every time, a foot high and never touching the ground, no trouble. But I thought it was the younger players who should be doing it, not me. I led by example and used to offer a penny to a pound in ten kicks if they could do it too. I collected quite a few pennies and never lost a pound. Another challenge was shooting from the halfway line into a five-a-side net placed in the goalmouth. And I introduced badminton, gymnastics and the vaulting-horse into training, the only sessions we did without a ball. Badminton is a great game for finesse, power and nimbleness. You really get a sweat on with two-a-side badminton, and it improves stamina, agility and coordination. The players told me their previous training regime largely consisted of running round the field. I attempted to use gymnastic skills to enhance athleticism. Going over a horse or springboard was aimed at getting players to be more agile on the football field. You'd have thought I was asking them to commit hara-kiri – asking them to get their feet off the floor and fly through the air. Yet within a month, they were jumping through hoops off the vaulting-horse. And their balance had improved 100 per cent. I told Walter Winterbottom that such techniques would come in eventually throughout the game, but no one was thinking about it at the time. As a Forces PTI and qualified FA coach – one of the first after the war – I was prepared to do anything to develop a player's skill.'

One of those things was the Newcastle players' brief flirtation with Highland dancing, one of the best-kept secrets of post-war soccer. Not a whisper got out to the press, as the United staff, to a man, saw it as one innovation too far – especially after the petticoat strip jibes.

'I tried it because I realised how tremendously it had helped me in my football. But after a month, I had to give up. When we started, you'd have thought they were shire horses trying to skip around the swords, bloody shire horses! Lads like Alf McMichael, Dick Keith, Lennie White, Ivor Allchurch,

George Eastham – but could they master it? Could they hell! I tried to convince them sword dancing was even better than jumping the springboard and the horse – and not as sissy as it sounds. But that was the problem. I started putting it to music, but they thought they looked too much like a bunch of sissies. They couldn't see the point I was making.

'If I was managing today, I would insist on players doing it. Never mind what anyone else thinks. You just need to put two crossed sticks on the ground, skip over them to music, moving your feet in and out, and you'll soon get a different person – your walking and your posture is improved and your balance is 100 per cent better. Balance in Highland dancing is magnificent. You can tell just by looking at how players move who has and who hasn't got perfect balance. You get the same energy and sweat out of Highland dancing as you'd get from running up and down the track. And it's not as boring because you've got to work with the other three boys, and your brain is flashing, thinking about the steps and moves.'

There were few other stories that were kept so quiet. Off the field, Mitten had come to realise that nothing creates public interest more than publicity, and he mercilessly set about exploiting the press's insatiable appetite for a good story, with or without a canine bent. Journalists were never stuck for a quote from Cheeky Charlie, and Newcastle could compete for the headlines with the biggest clubs in the country. But it was a high-risk as well as a high-profile strategy, and the 1958–59 season had barely got under way when Charlie got the first inklings of what was to come. The *Daily Mail* reported ominously: 'The poison gossip is already at work. Already there are signs that there are people at Newcastle who don't like and don't want to like Mitten's ideas. There are those on the board who are only too ready to sabotage Mitten or any other manager likely to disturb their hibernation.'

The fundamental problem at Newcastle was a long-running rivalry on the board between Alderman William

McKeag and two former chairmen, G. Stanley Seymour and Wilf Taylor. As manager, Seymour had guided the club to its post-war successes, and it seems clear that he regarded the manager's chair as his own in all but name. The *Daily Mail* commented: 'Mr Seymour was the inspiration of three Wembley triumphs, but, like a well-known television compère, always insists he's in charge. He has not been in charge this season and has taken on the role of sniper.'

McKeag and vice-chairman Wally Hurford, however, had decided that Mitten was the club's best hope. The result was almost continuous faction-fighting and closely split boardroom votes. Decisions were always knife-edged and continuity impossible because of a system of rotating the chairmanship, a key consideration because of a chairman's casting vote.

Charlie survived the first, proving season as Newcastle finished halfway up the table, and he demanded a new, four-year contract. It was the minimum time he felt was needed to implement his plan for total reorganisation at Gallowgate. McKeag argued in favour, and the Seymour faction opposed it. Instead, a one-year renewal was offered. It took a bit of background politicking by Charlie himself – and rumours of talks with Leeds United – to win the day for McKeag. But even then Charlie had to settle for three years – the same period as the chairmanship.

'When it came for my contract renewal, there was a merry dance. I'd kept them waiting during that first year, because I'd wanted another four years and total control over the team. I said I'd think about re-signing after one year. I had got a call from Leeds, who said they'd heard I was unhappy at Newcastle, and would I like to consider going to Elland Road. I arranged a meeting with Leeds chairman Sam Bolton and signed a contract for more than I was getting at Newcastle. But after I talked it over with McKeag, I felt I had let him down. So I telephoned Sam Bolton, and he agreed to cancel my Leeds contract.'

The first thing the board told Mitten after he'd re-signed was that there was only £20,000 in the kitty for transfers – despite his warning that more was needed for quality players to plug the gaps. So, the Mitten revolution was begun in earnest, and in 1960 Newcastle ended the season in eighth place, one below Manchester United. What is astonishing is how far ahead of its time Mitten's programme was: disengaging from reliance on 'star' players; boldly going for home-grown talent with a classroom to dressing-room youth policy; absolute priority given to skills development; supporting a rise in the minimum wage. Mitten regarded footballers as professional artists who should be rewarded as such, and he was uncompromising in demanding that his charges, for their part, refine and work at their own skills.

'I expected honest endeavour from my players and never asked them to do anything I couldn't demonstrate for them in training. My philosophy was simple: let the football do the talking. I used to set out half a dozen activities with the ball, in a circuit, based on football skills. I was trying to create natural habits that players would do without thinking on the field while playing the game. And do it right. Reflex footballing skills. And they started believing in themselves; if I spotted weaknesses, I would offer antidotes and show them how it should be done or how they could adapt a technique to their natural level of ability.

'The point about ball-work is to gain total mastery of the ball, to be able to tell it what to do and be able to stick it in the net as often as possible. I taught them my penalty technique. Eastham was our penalty-taker, but he never hit one right – like so many players today, he always side-footed it. But he could put a bit of power into it, and George's big asset was his accuracy. He could pass the ball very well and had good positional sense. In his stride, he used to run like a crab. But he could play. He and Lennie White were a very happy marriage on the field. If I had to give a sharp telling-off to anyone, that went for the lot; they all took note. I found all the players had respect for me. We had a good team spirit going there.' The *Newcastle Journal* summarised the Mitten regime thus:

> He has always urged that football should be played at all levels from schoolboy stage upwards, between March and November – when the skills of the game can be developed and practised along the lines which will enable Britain to match the abilities of other rising soccer nations . . . insisted that appreciably increased payments to top-class players was essential if the best material was to be drawn into professional football . . . that United's greatest prospect depended largely on concentrating on making players . . . and urged the adoption of an apprentice professional staff of lads in full-time training as an integral part of his nursery plan.

This looks uncannily like the Dutch side Ajax's 'total football' regime which has made the Netherlands one of the world's most exciting football nations. But there is an even more uncanny connection. Within a year of starting his youth policy, Charlie began taking the pick of his young players to Holland's international youth tournament in Amsterdam.

'We won it every year. I was on the right track, building a cracking team of young players. But most of the board couldn't see it at the time. Within weeks of my getting fired at Newcastle, my juniors won the FA Youth Cup – the only time they've won it. And who goes up to take the presentation but Stan Seymour!'

Charlie had never been one to pull his punches, and now that he was given the chance to put his own ideas into practice he was often impatient with those who failed to share his vision or whom he considered downright incompetent. As the *Daily Express* put it: 'The once cheeky Charlie is a dedicated man – if he doesn't like what he sees, he complains . . . about referees, about opposing teams, about anybody he does not see eye to eye with, because he is a perfectionist and because he still insists on saying his piece.'

Inevitably, he made enemies faster than he was able to bring success. That cracking team arrived too late to save Charlie's skin, but it is a measure of his policies that seven of his youth squad went on to become internationals and included such names as Alan Suddick (then hailed as the new Stanley Matthews), Bobby Moncur, George Graham and George Dalton.

Change is always unsettling and the big problem facing Charlie was that it affected results on the field. The solution was to buy in one or two ready-made quality players to help the first team through the rebuilding period while the youngsters came on stream. But it was in the transfer market that Charlie Mitten, although theoretically in absolute control over team affairs, was most vulnerable because the expenditure of transfer fees was subject to ratification by the whole board. As Charlie recalled it, his scouting expeditions became a game of cat and mouse – with his own directors. In two out of every three cases, what Mitten proposed, the board opposed. The result was a succession of players – later to become household names – whose signature Charlie missed. Thus, Denis Law, then a 17 year old at Huddersfield, was vetoed because he clearly didn't look strong enough to punch his way out of a paper bag. Charlie never forgot the boardroom discussion when he put Law's name forward: 'Wilf Taylor reported that Law had "brittle bones", and, in the opinion of the FA grapevine, he would not make it as a professional player.'

Similarly lost were George Herd of Clyde, scooped up by Sunderland after Mitten's hush-hush move for the player unaccountably leaked out (the trail led back to the St James' Park boardroom); Charlie Cooke of Aberdeen, who was considered not worth it at £20,000 (he ended up at Chelsea); and Jimmy Greaves, ditto at £25,000 (he decamped for AC Milan in an £80,000 deal, for a reputed £15,000 up-front cut and a £40,000 three-year contract).

One player Charlie was proud of having brought to the club was George Dalton, who became an England Under-21 player, but a bad leg injury cut short a promising career. George was later coach at Ipswich and a physio at Coventry City, where Charlie's grandson Paul spent time on the playing staff. Another who didn't get away was Ivor Allchurch, Swansea's immaculate Welsh international inside-forward. But it was a £10,000 coup shrouded in secrecy – so that Charlie's own board wouldn't foul up the deal.

'When I bought Ivor Allchurch, I had to do things the wrong way round – with skulduggery – and not tell the board what was going on; that's what it came to. Allchurch was then around 30, an international and a great player – ready for me. I'd rung Trevor Morris, the manager at Swansea, and we fixed everything up. I arranged for Allchurch to sign in Manchester – after a medical check by the physio at Old Trafford – before the game against Manchester City, which we won 3–2. I played my son John at outside-left that game. The "big five" boardroom opposition faction were at the England v. Scotland international at Hampden Park. When the score at Maine Road came across, I was told after, there was silence; they were expecting us to lose. My own directors wanted me to lose! It ended up being my team when we lost and theirs when we won.'

Mitten even remembers the board meeting on buying a player he had rejected. 'I was looking for another inside-forward and the opposition faction said, "How about the Liverpool player Jimmy Harrower, should we get him?" But I'd seen him play and told McKeag I didn't want anything to do with him. That same week, I was after a goalkeeper from Brighton who went on to be a Welsh international. We were around the boardroom table, and I banged the table and said, "I'm going to Brighton to sign Hollins; you and Mr Seymour can do what you like."

'So Seymour made the arrangements. We were playing Tottenham at White Hart Lane, and we stopped over at Peterborough. They signed the Liverpool lad at Peterborough railway station – the Liverpool junction between Newcastle and London. We played him at Tottenham, and you've never seen such an exhibition. I could have taken off my jacket and played better myself. It was the year Spurs won the League and Cup Double. We were beating them, and we ended up losing – Dave Mackay went over the top and broke Lennie White's leg: he was never the same again.'

The one player above all others Charlie Mitten regretted losing was Ian St John, then at Motherwell. 'I never signed anyone I hadn't seen play, and after watching St John a couple of times, I thought, boy, can this lad play. I saw in him another di Stefano – I was that impressed with his playmaking. I told the board I wanted to buy St John and move Lennie White to outside-right. I arranged to travel up to see St John. We agreed terms. As I was leaving, Bill Shankly was arriving in a taxi. Shankly says to me, "Oh, bloody hell, Charlie, are you here?" He'd come up himself to sign St John. I said, "Never mind, Bill, better luck next time." Back in Newcastle, I found the newspapers had been full of me going up to sign St John, and I'd told no one. Next day, I was determined to find out how it had got out. So I rung up a local reporter I knew who always talked straight. And he told me Stan Seymour had tipped him off before I'd even started out for Scotland to sign St John. That's how much Seymour and McKeag were at loggerheads. I was caught in the middle of a boardroom war.

'When I presented the contract to the board, they refused to sanction St John's transfer. The fee was £35,000, a lot of money in those days. But Newcastle had the money, and St

John was always going to be a great player. So the deal fell through, and Shanks, being Shanks, went straight back to sign St John.'

The way Ian St John tells it is that Charlie had talked persuasively about the advantages of joining Newcastle, who were a big club, whereas Liverpool were only in the Second Division. As a 22-year-old player, married with a young family and living in a tenement building not far from the Motherwell ground, St John was both flattered and impressed.

'I'd come back from a game, and Charlie was sitting in his car outside waiting for me. He came in and we had a chat about me coming to Newcastle, and he told me how to go about getting in a transfer letter. I was panicking – I was a kid, and in those days the players were tied to the club, and it was a very difficult thing to do. He said, "Don't worry, we'll smooth the way." It was all set up. After two or three attempts, my transfer request was finally granted by Motherwell. They were managed then by Bobby Ancell, an ex-Newcastle player himself. The amazing thing was the day I got the transfer granted, Bill Shankly arrived. We'd a game that evening and Bobby told me to hang on after. I was introduced to Shanks and we go straight in and talk money with him. He said we'd go to Liverpool the next day. It was a fait accompli. I was overwhelmed by it all. So I said, with Newcastle in mind, I must have time to think about it. As far as I was concerned, I didn't want to go to Liverpool because Newcastle were the big club. So Bobby Ancell says, "I'll tell you something, you're not going to Newcastle!" Charlie had thought his secret deal was kept under wraps. Bobby says, "Liverpool have come up here and done everything right, and I'd like to pretend I've never heard of Newcastle."

'As a kid, you think maybe the managers don't know what's going to happen – but they know everything that's going on. So that sort of put the hat on it. Next morning, Shanks comes up and picks up my wife and me, the baby and the dog, and we drive to the club in a Rolls-Royce. We deposited the baby and the dog at my mother-in-law's, and off we went down to Liverpool. I didn't see Charlie again for years.

'Later on, Jimmy Greaves told me Charlie had come to him as well to get him to sign. It's amazing to think it could have been Saint and Greavsie at Newcastle. To get Jimmy a few quid extra, Greavsie said Charlie had promised him a part-time job as a car salesman. He'd probably have had to go down to somebody's car place and stand there in the afternoon for an hour or so. I said to Greavsie, "He must have seen you as an Arthur Daley – I never got the offer of a car salesman's job!"'

Comparing the young Scots player to di Stefano was rather more of a compliment. For Charlie Mitten saw the Argentinian maestro, then orchestrating Real Madrid's total domination of European soccer, as the complete footballer – the master. And as the boardroom strife cast an ever more gloomy shadow over his managership at Gallowgate, there came a surprise reunion between the two Bogotá Bandits which was one of Charlie's fondest memories.

It happened during a summer tournament in Majorca. The Maestro, then 32 and at his brilliant best for Real Madrid, stepped out against Newcastle in the tournament. Di Stefano was guesting for the Spanish first-division side Mallorca, and Charlie was playing himself at outside-left for Newcastle. These pre-season tour games were the only occasions he turned out for the Magpies. So Charlie found himself crossing swords in a game for a final time with Real's extraordinary playmaker.

'It was a great moment – we recognised each other as soon as we ran out onto the field. Di Stefano was guesting during the off-season. The other teams, from all over Europe, included Feyenoord, Nuremberg and a Swedish team. He said, "*Meeten, Meeten*, you play like you play in Bogotá. OK, OK! But you no fat like me." So I said, "Steff, you had better

207

stop heading the ball, it's taking off all your hair." And he said, "Ah, *Char-lez*, but every hair is a goal, no?"

'Me at outside-left was the only change in our side – I'd moved Bobby Mitchell back to left-half. As it happened, di Stefano's team wasn't too good; and we beat them 3–1 and actually won the tournament. Coming off the field, he put his arm around me and said to McKeag, "This is *Char-lez Meeten, mi amigo!*" And McKeag, who spoke Spanish like he was Winston Churchill, drew himself up to his full height and said, "Alfredo, Charles my *amigo*, now you my *amigo!*"

'There is no doubt in my mind that di Stefano was the supreme playmaker. What he could do with the ball was unbelievable – he could almost hide it with his feet and leave a defender wondering where it was. He was a perfectionist, always striving to be better. I think Ian St John had those same skills – he could make people want to play. And because of that, it was always a great game of football because he made things happen.'

Back on Tyneside, the things Charlie Mitten had been making happen at Gallowgate finally exploded in the storm which was to end his League management aspirations forever. The failure to sign St John in April had been the last straw. 'I could buy a stinking player for £30,000, but I wasn't allowed to buy a good one for £10,000! That's what made me realise there was a real power game going on. I got the impression that the majority of the board didn't really want me to be there, taking the management of the club out of their hands. I was coming on strong. If I'd sided with the other faction, I'd probably still be at Newcastle.'

Then came the blow of relegation. Newcastle had gone down in 1961, partly as a result of the sweeping changes Charlie had instituted and partly because morale had dived as a result of the protracted George Eastham affair. Charlie nevertheless managed to survive the vote of confidence and was still in the manager's chair as the new season started in

September 1961. But the strain was beginning to tell at home.

'In the last few months at Newcastle, the pressures were affecting my wife and my whole family. We'd moved up there and made many good friends and found they were nice people on Tyneside. But it was the job that went all wrong. It became five days of bloody harassment every week.

'The board lost confidence in me – and I must say I lost heart. It was always the manager and the chairman against the rest of the board. Everything I did seemed to be wrong. Even when I changed the colour of the jersey, the directors didn't like it. Just look at the colours of jerseys today – blacks and blues and greens, and all sorts of combinations. I introduced hoops on the bottom of the shorts so players didn't have to keep looking up all the time in close play before passing, and it made them half a yard faster. That was the first time in England; it was revolutionary at the time. But it was only because I kept thinking about the game.

'Another thing I've long believed is that we should have goal judges to decide when a ball hits the bar and bounces down on the line, to say if it was over or not. Look at the famous England World Cup goal against West Germany. To this day, there are doubts whether it crossed the line. The Germans still say it didn't. In cricket, they use video evidence. I think video cameras monitoring play in football are a must – and it's inevitable they will come. An incident can be reviewed in an instant, a playback only takes seconds and would help referees to avoid making wrong decisions and stop arguments and unfairness – say, about a crucial penalty or a sending-off. It's important never to stop thinking about the game and not be afraid to make changes you think are necessary.

'I look back now on the ingredients required to be a top-class manager; I think you've got to be a jack of all trades. But the biggest recipe for success is that you've got to be able to be a Dr Jekyll and Mr Hyde to your own players – yes, even to the players at times. With my board of directors, I was always dead straight – I didn't care if they liked it or lumped it. But not with the players, and that's wrong. You can be blunt, nice and nasty, but I found you can't always talk straight, you've got to fiddle around a bit. I would size up a person and think, "If I give him a bollocking, will he turn it on for me on Saturday afternoon?"

And it was one player coming straight out and saying he wouldn't ever again be turning it on for Newcastle which sparked the contract revolution that had been simmering for ten years since the Bogotá affair.

His name was George Eastham.

# 15

# Revolution

Eastham will be shovelling coal before he's allowed to
leave Newcastle.

Newcastle United director Stan Seymour

WHEN THE BOGOTÁ STORM BROKE IN THE SPRING OF 1950,
Players Union chairman Jimmy Guthrie warned that the
soccer outlaws were 'blazing a trail and will be the first of
many British footballers to go abroad unless conditions
change. I have no doubt their action will benefit every player
in the country.' Brave and prophetic words, but they were not
to be fulfilled for ten years.

The truth was that the Union in the early 1950s was being
marginalised by an increasingly intransigent League as the
political climate changed (the Conservatives began a 13-year
period in office in 1951), and the austerity years gave way to
the affluent never-had-it-so-good society. Hopes for a new
'players charter' dissolved as the 1953 Foster Report
unexpectedly endorsed the maximum wage and even the
retain-and-transfer system. (The Government had set up the
Foster Inquiry as the Union repeatedly resorted to Ministry of
Labour arbitration to sort out its interminable wrangling with

the League.) And Guthrie's bid to toughen the Union's bargaining position by seeking a closed shop and affiliating to the TUC failed amid tactical differences in the union leadership, and star players seeking their own ways of beating the system, often with the contrivance of their clubs.

Thus, for players seeking better rewards who did not go abroad, there were ways around the restrictions on payments. Len Shackleton, Sunderland's magisterial inside-forward, never hid his view that a strike was the only way to get rid of the player's contract, which he described as an 'evil document'. But in the absence of any solidarity action, he – like many others – took care of himself through the proverbial brown envelope. Under-the-counter payments were nothing new – indeed, they had become an open secret. They had long been a duplicitous feature of the game as many clubs honoured their own rules more in the breach than the observance. The earnings rules were, of course, designed to keep what the League regarded as mere game-playing journeymen in their place. But many clubs found the restrictions counter-productive and, over the years, there were a number of celebrated cases where clubs were caught making illicit payments to players.

One of the earliest and most sensational was that of Manchester City in 1903, and involved the legendary Welsh international Billy Meredith. As a player, Meredith was a one-off. His slight frame and spindly legs belied a prodigious talent as an elusive, goal-scoring winger. Some have described him as the Best, Finney and Matthews of his day – all rolled into one. He won 51 caps – his last at the age of 45 – and played in an FA Cup semi-final when he was 50. He made his debut for Northwich Victoria before moving to Manchester City – and notoriety. In 1901, City (relegated the previous season), backed by newspaper millionaire Edward Hulton, swept back into the First Division and took the FA Cup for the first time.

The 'secret', according to Meredith, was that City 'put

aside the rule that no player receive more than £4 a week', the maximum permitted at that time. The following season he was suspended following match bribery allegations – which he vehemently denied. But at a subsequent inquiry, he admitted receiving under-the-counter payments. The FA all but disbanded City and an embittered Meredith joined his club's great rivals, Manchester United. He later complained to one reporter: 'They congratulate me and give me caps, but they will not give me a penny more than men in the reserve team.'

Meredith was determined to hit back at the committees of 'gentlemen' who had branded him an outlaw and treated him like a common thief, becoming a prime mover in the resurrection of the Players Union to fight for a better deal and a more honest and transparent system, for it was clear that many big clubs were making illicit payments. Middlesbrough, for example, were also fined for the same offence by the FA, only narrowly avoiding suspension. And in 1919, Leeds City – later Leeds United – were expelled from the League and their players 'auctioned off' to the highest bidder the following week.

And so it went on right up until the 1950s, until the last great pre-revolution payments scandal broke in 1957, the so-called 'Sunderland affair'. A joint FA–League inquiry confirmed what was common knowledge: illicit payments involving thousands of pounds going back years. It resulted in heavy fines for the club and the suspension of the directors. Roker Park's creative accounting was merely the tip of the iceberg. By then, few top clubs were not involved in such payments, but for the majority of players, who didn't benefit from this blatant breaking of the rules, the revelation of such duplicity was often a source of great bitterness.

Charlie recalled his feelings when the wills of the Manchester United players killed at Munich were published.

'Matt Busby's Babes were being paid more than the officially permitted maximum. I was raging when I saw it. And

I thought to myself, "There was the boss when I was at United giving us a two-bit tale that he could not pay us any extra, and we'd say fair enough, because he'd lose his job." You wouldn't ask your own manager to hang himself, would you? And it works out later that he's bought seven or eight youngsters and they were getting thousands in signing-on fees. These were illicit payments, bungs to the lads he was bringing in to Manchester United.

'When I played at United – and this is the gospel truth as the Lord is my judge – in that post-war team we never got a bean extra from Busby, even when we got to the FA Cup final. The only thing extra I ever got from Manchester United was three-or four-pound spends Busby would give us on tours – but that was allowed by FA rules. After the Munich air crash, those boys' bank accounts showed that they had far more than they could possibly have earned officially in their wages. Why didn't the club just play it straight? It was because the game was being run by a bunch of bloody amateurs. They should have put everything above board. When everybody has freedom of contract, you'll get a better quality of football, better international stars – and they'll finish with top wages anyway, whether you do it legally or illegally. So why not do it above board straight away? I couldn't have cared less if someone wanted to pay me a million – they must have thought I was worth it.'

The sweeping away of the discredited maximum wage came too late for Charlie as manager or player – indeed, it was his former Fulham teammate Johnny Haynes who became Britain's first £100-a-week footballer, a publicity master stroke by Fulham chairman Tommy Trinder. But there was no immediate big money free-for-all. Haynes's salary was the exception which proved the rule. (When Stan Matthews returned to Stoke City from Blackpool in a blaze of publicity in 1961, he got half that – even though his first home game attracted 35,000, compared to 8,000 the previous week.)

But the pay breakthrough was a revolution and came as the result of the emergence of a rejuvenated Players Union – now renamed the Professional Footballers Association. Under the dynamic leadership of Fulham inside-forward Jimmy Hill, the PFA had pursued a determined campaign on behalf of five Sunderland players made scapegoats in the fallout of the Roker payments scandal. The Sunderland men had been suspended *sine die* for refusing to testify before an FA–League inquiry. Hill's new union team discovered that the inquiry had all the legality of a kangaroo court, and the suspensions were later overturned and compensation paid for loss of wages. On the back of this success, Hill, who emerged as a master of public relations, launched a full-scale assault on the player's contract.

It is perhaps difficult today for players and fans alike to comprehend the meagre rewards that even the greatest stars played for just 50 years ago. In 1960, the most any professional footballer could earn was a maximum of £20 a week, £17 in the summer close season. But most could only dream about even those modest figures – it was estimated that no more than 20 per cent of players actually got the maximum. And, of course, all players were tied to their clubs for life by the retain-and-transfer contract system. The PFA's three key demands were abolition of the maximum wage, fairer contracts and a more equitable transfer system in which players would get a cut of the fee. The League's response of £2 a week on the maximum wage – and nothing else – was seen by observers like Charlie Mitten as little short of incredible.

'As a player, I would have loved to have had freedom of contract. But from the clubs' point of view, at the time, I didn't think this sudden ending of the system was necessarily a good thing. I believe the League could have controlled the spiralling wage bills that came after, had they had the foresight to loosen contracts in a measured way – to the benefit of all 92 clubs. They'd had the opportunity to say, when I came back from Bogotá, "Yes, Mr Mitten, the First Division *maximum* will be, say, £400, the Second £300, the Third £200 and the Fourth will be £100." They could have offered higher limits for stars, and the other players would have accepted that. They could have controlled the outlay of money in football, and, up to a point, that might have been a good thing.

'The clubs could have agreed to improve it as they went along, year by year, when they saw what level of cash was coming in at the turnstiles through bigger gates. Not every club could afford £400 a week, but the top players could have negotiated up to that limit. So the less-well-off clubs would have survived better. Players don't want to play for third- and fourth-division sides – they want to be up there where the cash is. I said to the FA disciplinary committee when I was up in front of them, "You're missing the opportunity of a lifetime to control salaries." But all they were interested in hearing from me was how much I had made in Colombia – and I wouldn't tell them! I said, "What's it got to do with you?" That's why I never played football for England again.

'Today, I do believe that the top-class player should get a top-class salary, and there should be total freedom of contract. If a club wants to pay a player £10,000 [or £20,000, or £30,000] a week, they must be able to afford it. No one's forcing them. You cut your coat according to your cloth.'

In January 1961, the PFA, having wrong-footed the League and its negotiators with a mixture of tough bargaining and astute use of publicity, prepared to go on strike. But with just hours to go, and having lost the public-opinion battle hands down, the League capitulated. The maximum wage was abolished and League negotiators conceded a modest modification to the retain-and-transfer system. It really amounted to only a marginal improvement in favour of the players, but it was seen as a crucial breakthrough.

Under the new contract, a player who refused to re-sign in the May of each year (to ensure his summer wages) would immediately be placed on the transfer list and enquiries invited from other clubs. If there was no progress by the August, the matter would be resolved by the League management committee. But crucially, unlike before, he would still be paid, albeit at the minimum rate for his division. Even this was too much for the most reactionary elements in the League, and it would take the full-blown legal challenge of the Eastham case finally to outlaw England's last vestiges of feudalism.

To everyone but club chairmen, it seemed, the wage revolution had been inevitable; an increasing number of top players were being lured away to Continental clubs, particularly Italian, for the kind of riches which had beckoned the Bogotá Bandits in 1950. John Charles in 1957 had been followed by others disillusioned with the crumbs offered by British clubs: Hibs' Joe Baker went to Turin for £73,000 and was followed by Denis Law for £100,000. The Milan clubs weren't far behind, Inter paying £80,000 for Gerry Hitchens and AC the same for Jimmy Greaves. The Chelsea goal-poacher's deal was £15,000 upfront plus a £40,000 three-year contract. To players and fans back home, such sums seemed almost unimaginable.

Although the clubs bowed to the inevitable over wages, they couldn't bring themselves to loosen the shackles of soccer serfdom. When the deal was taken back to the League's AGM in the summer for ratification, the clubs reneged on it. While the abolition of the maximum wage was allowed to stand, the new clause on contracts was not. League president Joe Richards told an extraordinary meeting of the League management committee: 'Come what may, the Football League will not alter the retain-and-transfer system.'

The way was now open for the court action which would vindicate the stand taken by Charlie Mitten when he set out on the road to Bogotá ten years earlier. And the wheel had come full circle for Mitten, who would find himself defending the very system which had condemned him to the status of an outlaw and frozen him out of international honours.

George Eastham was already at Newcastle when Mitten took over in June 1958. The player was a slightly built, cultured inside-forward who, as Charlie recalled, could make space and beat a man without looking as if he was trying. He had been signed from Ards in Northern Ireland and soon made his mark at St James' Park. In April 1960, however, he refused to sign a new contract for the next season (to ensure his summer wages) and requested a transfer. As ever, the root cause of Eastham's dispute was money. Charlie's own sense of *déjà vu* was overwhelming.

'At that time, football was in a state of unrest – players knew that they were not getting a salary to compensate for their professionalism, not getting the rewards for their skills. George said he felt he was not getting enough. Press speculation was that he had been tapped by an Arsenal agent, but I said I'd had no official approach from Arsenal. I didn't want him to go – he was one of my top players. But I couldn't offer him any more inducements. Arsenal couldn't officially have paid him more on his wages – he was getting the limit with us. But Arsenal could have given him a sizeable signing-on fee, as well as perks.

'I could understand the young lad's point that he was in the game only a set number of years to earn as much as he could get: "I'm one of the good players and I want my worth in the short time I've got." I'd felt exactly the same before I went to Bogotá – now I was on the management side, so I understood both arguments. The League never understood this. They just saw the players as cattle to be discarded, disposed of, as the club pleased.

'It wasn't necessarily that Eastham felt that Arsenal were a better or more glamorous club than Newcastle. It was just a case of getting better financial rewards. The only way George could better himself, with players' conditions at that time, was by moving. The negotiations reached stagnation point, and, in the summer, he went to the PFA. He just wanted to move, and the club came to the conclusion that what he really wanted was freedom of contract.'

Eastham's appeal to the League management committee in July was flatly rejected, the committee ruling the matter was solely the concern of club and player. Indeed, the affair was marked by acrimony and the intemperate attitude of some Newcastle directors, one of whom famously declared that Eastham would be shovelling coal before he was allowed to quit the club.

The PFA saw the affair as the perfect opportunity to challenge the legality of the retain-and-transfer system, and issued a writ alleging that Newcastle were acting in unlawful restraint of trade by preventing Eastham from earning a living playing football. In the event, Newcastle didn't even bother to answer the writ. Before the case could proceed, the club decided to wash its hands of Eastham by accepting an Arsenal bid of £47,000 for the player – not far short of the British transfer record set in March that same year when Manchester City paid £50,000 to Huddersfield for Denis Law. As Mitten recalled, it was money that talked loudest for the Newcastle board.

'The fans might say, "You sold one of our best players," but they [the board] could reply, "But we got a near-record fee for him." The transfer market had rocketed, and the board seemed more concerned with the fee than defending the retain-and-transfer system, which they assumed would go on. My board wasn't interested in the contract dispute. I didn't want Eastham to go, but what could I do if he wouldn't play for me? All I could do was keep him out of football by not signing his transfer. I had nothing personal against the lad. He was principled and acted perfectly honourably. He played it straight – and he was a brilliant player for me, an automatic selection at Newcastle, and deservedly went on to be an international. But as regards to earning money, the only way open to him was what he did.'

Eastham signed for Arsenal in early November 1961. But Mitten's signature wasn't on the transfer forms. An extraordinary secret meeting had already sealed the fate of Cheeky Charlie, the revolutionary soccer manager.

# 16

# Victory and Defeat

The retain-and-transfer system is an unjustifiable restraint
of trade where the employers have succeeded in setting
up a monolithic front throughout the world.

Lord Justice Wilberforce, 4 July 1963

THE HIGH COURT DECLARATION THAT A LEADING ENGLISH
football club was acting outwith the law in operating the
retain-and-transfer system was, according to the *Daily Mail*,
the biggest bombshell ever to hit soccer. But by then, Charlie
Mitten, named in the court action along with the FA, the
Football League, Newcastle United and its directors, was long
gone from St James' Park. He'd been sacked in a classic
boardroom coup 18 months earlier – but to his immense
discomfit had had to maintain intimate contact with his
former employers as they defended the legal action to which
he was a reluctant party and which he had warned the club
repeatedly that they would lose.

The graphic details of the six-day hearing made for a media
feeding frenzy as the newspapers vied to dramatise the
absurdities of a 70-year-old employment system – rooted in
the Middle Ages – which was being forensically taken apart in

court. At one point, Eastham's counsel pungently observed that a football club was the only limited company which paid a lot of money for an asset it did not enter in a balance sheet. 'If a club bought an expensive head of cattle, that would have to appear as an asset. I do not know whether it is from a sense of delicacy or some process of law, which I have not discovered, that the same does not apply to players.'

'Soccer Slavery' and 'Players Treated Like Cattle' were among the more restrained headlines. What are less well known are the inner thoughts of a man who had to go into court to defend what he believed to be the indefensible, to try to justify what he himself had challenged as unjustifiable just ten years earlier.

'I advised Newcastle that the issues of freedom of contract, as being pursued by the PFA through the courts, would be accepted in law. And when it did get to court, Eastham's counsel made a brilliant case against what was described as slavery and player serfdom of the retain-and-transfer system.

'In all these years of stagnation, it was the Players Union who had let the players down, failed to challenge the issue in the courts. But it was also stupidity by the people at the top – the clubs who refused to accept that those who were doing the job should be given more consideration. I think it's great that players have freedom of contract and can earn £10,000 [and more] a week.

'But there were 50 or 60 top-class players in this country in my day who didn't benefit from this freedom and who were happy to turn it on just the same for £15 a week. Stan Matthews was one. If there was anyone who deserved such rewards, it was him. There were far more players in my day who were worth this kind of money, but didn't get it. Today, there are nowhere near that number. Those running the game were blind, living in the past, and when things began changing on the field, they couldn't see that either. I reminded the board of my position when I went to Bogotá. That I had taken

KC's advice then, and was told I would win my case.'

To be fair, Mitten's certainty was not shared by the PFA, and a satisfactory legal outcome was by no means guaranteed, as John Harding points out in his entertaining and perspicacious account of the case in his PFA official history, *For the Good of the Game*. But Charlie's uncompromising advice to the Newcastle board came from the heart – and from bitter experience. Though the PFA pay breakthrough was hailed as a great victory, the retain-and-transfer system was still, essentially, in place when the new season opened in 1961. After the League had reneged on the deal, frantic mediation efforts by the government's labour conciliators had failed to resolve the dispute. The deal agreed by League negotiators had been disowned by the clubs who trotted out the hoary old arguments about the need for safeguards against poaching and players holding clubs to ransom.

As the headline writers excoriated 'the League that died of shame', conciliators continued their efforts, with the League adamantly insisting that the retain-and-transfer system would remain the cornerstone of contractual arrangements with players until a court decided it was unlawful. The PFA, under the astute leadership of Cliff Lloyd (who had taken over from Jimmy Hill), sensed their opportunity. It was to Eastham's credit that, although happy to be playing again with a new club and reluctant to pursue his quarrel with Newcastle, he allowed the PFA to continue with the test case. And so the retain-and-transfer system was finally tested at law and found to be wanting.

Lord Justice Wilberforce's historic ruling came as a bittersweet verdict for Charlie Mitten – he was a losing party to the action – but the principle on which he'd set out for Bogotá had been vindicated. By then, though, he'd decided to put League football management behind him forever after his sudden sacking by Newcastle with eight months of his contract still to run. (He never forgot, and to his dying day claimed Newcastle still owed him eight months' salary.) The common wisdom, reflected throughout the press, was that relegation had been the reason, but there was more to it than that. After all, the board's decision to sack him had not been taken on a split vote – his dismissal had been unanimous, albeit in the absence of McKeag.

Only a few months earlier, Charlie had seen which way the wind was blowing in another stormy boardroom row. He'd been accused of making irregular payments to sign a teenage prospect playing junior football in Scotland. 'They said I bunged a young player to sign for us, but, in fact, I paid his club £250. He was an amateur, and it was legit to pay a transfer fee for him to sign for Newcastle. My board said it was illegal. But they knew what I was doing; it was all in the books. They'd signed the cheque.'

Charlie finally decided he'd had enough. Both his sons were on Newcastle's books, and, believing he couldn't survive the start of the new season, he arranged to have John transferred. At the beginning of August 1961, John, then 20, accepted a two-month trial at Leicester. The younger son, Charlie, jun., was an apprentice and not so vulnerable. (Giving John his first-team debut at Newcastle was one of Charlie's toughest decisions. 'I'd been wanting to play him at outside-left in the first team, but it was a really hard thing to do. But I was determined and said, "Right, lad, you've got it now, go and show them!" He scored one goal and made another, and the crowd took to him – you could hear them go oooh when he gave a good pass or crossed it, and you knew he was in, knew he was going to be all right.')

In September 1961, the Magpies had begun their first Second Division campaign for 13 years in disastrous fashion. The *Daily Mail* reported 'violent protests from the fans on the running of the club's affairs and team matters' despite Mitten's continued pleas that his policies would take time to bear fruit and amid widespread criticism, much of it orchestrated by hostile board factions. And in yet another close-run thing, the board voted 5–3 to back their embattled manager. The key influence once again had been Alderman William McKeag, who, in three and a half years, had never wavered in his support of Mitten.

The poor start to the season inevitably hit morale, and as Newcastle slumped to the bottom half of the Second Division, several players put in transfer requests. This was too much for the anti-Mitten faction at Gallowgate. The board decided to act – and unilaterally declared that no player would be released for international duty following the team's disastrous early performances. Welsh international Ivor Allchurch immediately resigned the captaincy, while another Welsh star, Ken Leek, who had only been signed in the close season for £25,000, joined the transfer-seekers. Wildly imaginative press accounts of the final days of Charlie Mitten's reign go a long way to explaining why even McKeag's allies on the board turned against their manager.

The players responded by winning their next two games – the first victories of the campaign – and demanding a showdown with the club's directors. The board agreed. On Friday, 13 October 1961, behind closed doors at St James' Park, the board faced a delegation of senior players led by Charlie Mitten. Only two directors were missing: McKeag and Wilf Taylor. Mutiny was in the air, and Charlie was not playing Captain Bligh. With Wally Hurford taking the chair, the players' delegation put forward five key proposals for serious consideration by the board: that the ban on international duty be lifted and players be released for their respective countries if called up; that action be taken to staunch the flow of leaks from Gallowgate which were helping to fuel morale-damaging stories in the press; that accommodation be provided at St James' park for the sole use of players' wives and families; that overnight hotel stays be arranged for all matches in the London area, rather than the team travelling back after the game, and that the club pay for an evening's entertainment; and that each player receive an increased allocation of FA Cup-final tickets. These demands may seem modest by today's standards, but in agreeing that they should be considered, Charlie Mitten was signing his own managerial death warrant. This enlightened attitude was surely the real reason for his dismissal.

Events now moved to their inevitable climax. The club's AGM was scheduled for 31 October, and it was common knowledge that McKeag had left for a two-week visit to America on 10 October. Within a week of his departure, a secret board meeting was called at which all seven other directors were present. The first team had won all their last three matches. The last, a 7–2 defeat of Bury, with five home-grown players in the line-up, was the biggest away win since Mitten had taken over. But this remarkable turnaround in the team's fortunes was not on the agenda: Charlie's future was. They voted 7–0 for the immediate termination of his contract.

One shareholder in the McKeag camp condemned the decision as 'infamous'. Wing-Commander Jimmy Rush, who cabled the news to McKeag in America, warned the board that Mitten, one of the most enlightened managers in football, had been dedicated to improving standards not only at Newcastle but in football generally. 'The young players he has found have just begun to click. His dismissal could not have come at a worse time.'

Charlie's recollection was that the 'hush-hush' showdown meeting of 13 October was supposed to be strictly confidential, yet within weeks of his sacking, details were being leaked to the press by the anti-Mitten faction on the board. 'Whether the points raised by the players were justified or not was not the issue. You'd never have believed the kind of stuff that was being reported about Newcastle at that time. They were leaking things just to do the manager down, that was all. They wanted to get rid of me and were trying to put me in a bad light. The papers ended up printing virtually everything.'

It is clear now that the Gallowgate leak machine went into overdrive to provide *ex post facto* justification for Mitten's sacking. Protests from his supporters were to no avail. The Bogotá Bandit had finally been blown out of League soccer for good.

# 17

# Power Rangers

The British were a tough-tackling rigid formation, their opponents full of individual flair and imagination.

BBC correspondent, Belize, 1966

TIME FOR A CONFESSION. IT IS NOT OFTEN THAT OUT OF THE blue you meet a kindred spirit from a completely different walk of life – and from another generation. In Charlie Mitten, this writer found such a soul. Until I started out on this quest for the Bogotá Bandit, I'd never heard of Cheeky Charlie. But in unravelling the details of an extraordinary career, I have teased out a simple philosophy of soccer that correlates exactly with my own dimly held belief about the game during more than 20 years as an amateur player, first in North Wales junior football with Holywell Town, Mostyn YMCA and Buckley Wanderers, and then in local Saturday and Sunday leagues in Chester and the Manchester area. Dimly held, because I never gave much thought to the finer, more theoretical points of a game first mastered in endless 20-a-side school playground sessions with a tennis ball and later played instinctively in W-formation 11-a-side matches.

As a schoolboy, my abiding memory is of oft-shouted

touchline advice to 'Get rid of it! Don't hog the ball!' My irritation was compounded by amazement – after all, wasn't that the opposite of what forwards, especially wingers, were supposed to do? I ignored the touch judges' verdict, of course, had fun with the ball and won county schoolboy honours. Running with the ball also wins matches, but it seems to have become a forbidden art for a generation of football coaches.

Later, during the days of England's 1966 World Cup success, like the hundreds of thousands of others who preferred to play rather than watch, I was pleasantly surprised at the national team's success. England had got a decent manager, and her luck had changed. The thought that England might be technically inferior to other countries didn't enter my head. It was just that somehow 'they' weren't picking the best players to beat those damn foreigners. (That Ramsey's predecessors might have had problems of their own, similarly, didn't occur to an outsider like me.) Unsophisticated, of course.

I also felt I was playing every week with other young amateurs who were potentially world-beaters, and that it would be only a matter of time before they were discovered by the big-city scouts. Obviously a very optimistic assessment. But there were then – indeed still are – many undiscovered gems out there among the 1.5 million amateurs who turn it on week after week on the nation's parks and recreation grounds who could make the grade in League soccer. I personally knew one or two who were invited for trials – but there were many, many more who certainly merited a look and weren't even approached.

Furthermore, I cannot remember any soccer-skills coaching at school or at any of the clubs I subsequently played for. You either had it or you didn't. So, today, is anyone looking for that young talent – without a cheque book – and are things any better in our schools and youth clubs? Indeed, do those who coach our youthful players really know either what they're looking for or what they're doing? Charlie Mitten's verdict in 1995 was a resounding no, but today Cheeky Charlie would have been pleasantly surprised by the efforts of fellow visionaries like Sir Trevor Brooking, once of West Ham and England. They are finally addressing the issues Charlie had been raising for 40 years.

'So many clubs looking for talent don't find it because they can't see it. All they can see are aeroplanes up in the sky and the ball flying alongside them. And ten giants running around beneath. You know why? Because they're unsure of their jobs, they're afraid, scared stiff of losing. They see the only way to get success is by keeping a clean sheet and getting one goal for a win. It's easier to destroy than be creative – that's the defender's motto for this kind of play, encouraged by such coaches and managers. It may get them to the top of their division, but who wants to watch that sort of stuff? No wonder gates in the lower divisions are so low. Today's crowds are a new generation. They can watch other countries' teams on TV, and they think, "Why can't our players play like that?" If they see it at their own club, they'll go again.

'Busby's tactics at Old Trafford were to bring on young players, taking three years to mature. I did exactly the same at Newcastle and had scouts all over the North-East. They were part-timers, some were ex-footballers, but the main thing was that they knew what they were looking for. A good scout is the most important man in the football world. I picked them personally and had them down to St James' Park for a seminar before each season. You've got to trust your scouts – they're your eyes and ears. There's a big grapevine in football, of course, but it's up to the scout to follow up and report on promising youngsters.

'At United, Matt had Jimmy Murphy and Bert Whalley – Bert was his scout for the whole area of Lancashire. He was a godsend for United. An ex-United player, a wing-half, he knew his football and was a gentleman. He had a nice approach with mums and dads – he could break the ice with them and talk them into allowing their son to come down to see the United set-up. That was in the days when they were just another ordinary club and people needed persuading.'

Today, a vital change in our approach to coaching at the most junior levels does finally seem to be filtering through via the UK's various football associations. Cheeky Charlie Mitten might have said: 'Not before bloody time!'

Looking back, our roles as young players were mapped out for us psychologically long before we pulled on the third, second or first XI school jersey. Our game-play was informed by a positional mindset that ran something like this: wingers go down the wing and cross the ball; inside-forwards are midfield conveyor belts who run up and down the field all day from box to box; a centre-forward is big and tough and bustles around their box, scoring with his head and either foot; wing-halfs win the ball and distribute it to the forwards; a centre-half stops the opposing team's clever players and clogs the ball (and them, if necessary) away to clear the lines; and full-backs never take opposing wingers prisoners and boot the ball as far up the touchline as possible.

Once an 11 year old was assigned to one of these roles, he grew into the part, functioning as to the manner born. Switching roles was difficult enough, but actually changing the essentials was almost unheard of. So a boy assigned as centre-half (central defence, as we call it today) or full-back (defenders in general) was not expected to be able to dribble. Rugged, strong and fit, yes; creative, no. The physical size of the young player invariably determined his future in football – whether at amateur or professional level. Ball juggling was for forwards – and those who insisted on hogging the ball were put out on the wing where they could do the least damage to their own side's cohesion and teamwork. 'Who do you think you are – Stanley Matthews?' (or, later, 'George Best?') was one of the more charitable jibes, I constantly heard from the touchline. But where are the home-grown ball artists today?

This division of labour has a long dishonourable tradition going back at least 50 years. Thus, Neil Franklin said the real reason why he went to Bogotá was his 'desperate desire' to get away from Stoke City because of the way he was expected to play. He had a fundamental difference of opinion with City's manager at the time, Bob McGrory. Indeed, it was only after Stoke had refused even to consider Hull City's £30,000 bid – which would then have been a transfer record – that Franklin realised he was trapped and would have to take drastic action.

Franklin's unique style as a defender made him England's automatic choice at centre-half for four seasons after the war. But as he later joked 'it gave Bob McGrory heart attacks'. At Stoke, they wanted him to boot the ball away, get rid of it as quickly as possible. But he refused to be just a crude 'stopper' centre-half. As he said in his autobiography: 'I've never been able to understand why I should be expected to hurt a fellow player. Any lout can knock a man off the ball – it needs a footballer to take it off an opponent.'

Franklin was that rare exception – an English defender who was neither brutal nor mechanistic and who was absolutely comfortable on the ball. No wonder the South Americans welcomed him with open arms – they could recognise a kindred spirit. When the Hungarians and then the Brazilians exploded onto the world scene in the 1950s, all received wisdom about the game which England gave the world went out the window. A few sagely nodded their heads and thought there might be something in having ten players who could beat a man or two. And as Charlie Mitten argued for more than 40 years, the English game learned nothing and forgot nothing.

Tradition, it seems, does indeed die hard. Certainly as recently as ten years ago, the BBC clearly believed that those so quintessentially English W-formation skills were alive and well from the bottom up in English soccer. In January 1996, in its *From Our Own Correspondent* programme, a never less than entertaining pot-pourri of life in far-off places, the Beeb's man was reporting from Belize. The tiny Central American country is one of the few remaining outposts of the empire and has a British garrison which, not unnaturally, has a football team. And in a game against their hosts, the Army lads were said to have displayed the usual English traits of 'rigid formation and tough tackling', while the soccer of their native opponents was 'full of flair and imagination'.

If that seems like anecdotal evidence, it is more than backed up by the facts. In a seminal report a year before the BBC report, the Professional Footballers Association identified a key problem as an obsession with 'big is beautiful' at the most junior level of the game: schools soccer.

In an interview with me, Paul Power, then of the PFA coaching secretariat, spelled out the issues. He has since moved on to Manchester City's Academy coaching staff, but it's worth rehearsing his analysis made back in 1995: 'The problem has been the philosophy with which we approach the game from eight-year-old level, playing 11-a-side football on great big pitches with great big goals which their dads are going to play on in the afternoon. And you end up putting on your strongest player at centre-half, because if you're going to score at the other end, it's that far away you've got to kick it so hard to get the ball into their area. You see this in schoolboy games, and it's the natural thing to do. But in every country on the Continent, without exception, they play seven-a-side, across the pitch. So you end up with 28 players, 14 in each half, all getting more touches of the ball.

'The Dutch have a philosophy of four versus four, so they mark out five areas on a normal-sized pitch, and they'll play four players against four with different aspects of the game in mind. So, they'll have a game with four goals, two for each side to attack, which teaches you awareness, how to switch play, how to pass the ball, play diagonally, as a defender as well, because you've got two goals to look after. In another, they'll have five small pitches on one big pitch and they rotate the players – and results don't mean anything.

'It means that you get lots of touches of the ball, as you're only playing four-a-side at a time. You've got this diamond shape which gives you length, width and depth in your team so all the elements of football are there. So it's no wonder they are developing better players than us.

'In our scenario, if you're playing 11 players in a team, the left-winger might only get three touches of the ball in each half, or even the whole game, so he's only got three decisions to make. So he's not going to learn very quickly what is right and what is wrong. If you play seven versus seven and you get fifteen touches of the ball, you're soon going to learn to choose the right options. With seven-a-side, players are going to be up front one minute, wide the next, and they might be defending after that, so it develops a more complete player. You can't afford to be resting for a minute.

'On our big-pitch scenario, you tend to get one-on-one situations. In the centre-forward versus the centre-half, if the former is quick, he might knock it past the defender, and that's it – the latter is not really developing a whole-game mentality. He's become a stopper, with No. 5 on his back, and that's his position until he contacts a pro club who might then make some decisions about whether he's better at midfield, or upfront, or whatever. The point is we don't develop complete players, whereas they do on the Continent.

'And in a fairly recent innovation, they've started doing this at the age of five – because they don't think they're developing technically gifted players any more. Their whole idea is that if they can strengthen the base of competent players, the ones that rise to the top will be excellent and there'll be more of them.'

In their groundbreaking report, the Manchester-based PFA

made a number of recommendations, the most radical being that all home FAs introduce small-pitch games for seven-a-side teams for all football teams up to the age of 13. This has long been the practice in Argentina, where boys don't play 11-a-side games until they're 14. The South Americans believe that 11-a-side soccer tends to be dominated by bigger and stronger boys, thereby deterring the development of skilful players.

First to take such radical change on board has been the Welsh FA, which has completed the switch-over begun throughout Wales in 1994. Mini-football began to be introduced on a rolling basis, starting with eight year olds, for all primary schools playing affiliated football on either Saturdays or Sundays. The new system includes small goalmouths and non-competitive fixtures. The new rules are mandatory, and although it has been a logistics nightmare organising and funding the change-over, even the most sceptical observers who initially opposed the switch have been convinced.

According to Jimmy Shoulder, then (1996) coaching director of the Welsh FA, the big initial problem was to get qualified coaches in place in every area to oversee the programme. 'Give it time to bed in and come back in five or six years, and we'll be asking why we never played this way before. We're so old-fashioned and so far behind current thinking that, where once we led the world, we're now being dragged along behind.'

The hope is that more children will be encouraged to play and more talent will emerge – as has been the case in young footballing nations like Australia and Japan, who have made big strides in teaching techniques over the past two decades. Jimmy Shoulder knows from first-hand experience that it can work – he was Australia's national coach for ten years. And Oz is producing players who can hold their own at the highest level in Europe.

Today (2005), all Welsh junior school soccer is played under the mini-pitch protocol, with encouraging results, according to the Welsh FA's Mark Evans. 'It applies to pretty much every primary school. Every child below secondary school level – whether in infant school or primary school – plays mini-football in their schools. It can be five-a-side, six, seven, even eight-a-side, depending on the age of the players and the size of the pitch they are using.

'We have them playing on special small pitches where they have lots of touches of the ball, lots of involvement . . . keeping it a bit of fun, to be honest . . . just so they enjoy it, until they get to the age of 12, and then we get on with the serious stuff.

'It will take a few years before it comes to fruition. Obviously, we are still waiting for that. But we've some good players coming through our youth ranks. They are home-grown. So, we believe our system is working.'

However, the English FA have not gone so far down this road, though they have made a start. Over the last four years, there has been a significant increase in mini-soccer for kids under 12, with a lot more coaching now at the youngest level. 'Basically the aim is to put the emphasis on two things – enjoyment and technique,' says the FA's Andrin Cooper. 'And we now have a far more formalised structured coaching qualification.'

On the key issue of coaching, the FA's approach has been energised by Sir Trevor Brooking, says Cooper. 'The idea is we wanted to get training to a good level, with the maximum number of coaches possible, so that any children or adults who wanted to get involved in the game at the lowest level, or whatever level they play at, have access to good-quality coaching. And that goes alongside the money we are investing in the grassroots to improve the facilities and other things.

'We want to raise standards across the board, at the grassroots level, on the basis that, if we're getting things right at the age where children are a) developing their love for the game and b) honing their technique, it's going to improve things at the top end of the game. And that's very much been Trevor Brooking's mantra – we need to improve technique, let's say, in the eight to ten-year-old bracket . . . controlling the ball, manipulating the ball, passing . . . that's really the window to hone those skills.

'Trevor has also been quite vocal that the whole attitude of the game has to be different. And I suppose the issue comes down to the behaviour of parents on the sidelines. You know, that children should be encouraged to express themselves without fear of being verbally admonished, that as well as good technique being encouraged, poor technique should not be.

'Basically it's having people who are properly qualified to teach technique as well as all the other things that are important for the passions of the game – the teamwork and everything.

'Trevor B is really on the ball. Looking at the performances of our youth teams over the last two years, we are certainly seeing that the players who went into the academy from the beginning – eight or seven years ago now – are now breaking into first teams. Now we can start to see the fruit of the academy system.'

It was Charlie's fervent belief that without such a concerted attempt by the biggest home associations to learn from the successful footballing nations – many with only a tenth of the population of England – English soccer would always struggle to catch up with the rest of the world.

Poor coaching regimes based on mechanistic principles and statistical analyses – such as how many passes on average it take to score a goal – were also partly to blame for England's lack of success internationally, but not entirely, according to Paul Power.

'It's not all down to the direct-play strategy, although that has not contributed massively to the development of visionary midfield players. But it has certainly contributed to the style of play we have in England. In defence, we've always been encouraged to hit the ball forward as early as possible, and not run it out from defence the way the Dutch, Germans, Italians and the Brazilians – in fact, everyone else except us – do. We have been aware at the top level in England of the type of football these countries are playing, but we've been insular in our approach to playing. We've thought no one has anything to teach us.'

Power's argument is that there are times when direct play is appropriate and times when it is not. But deciding whether to play a long-ball or a short-passing game depends on having the players – and that means defenders, too – who are comfortable on the ball and are technically able to make that choice. But you can count on the fingers of one hand the number of such defenders in English soccer over the years. Very, very few. Neil Franklin and, more recently, Scotland international Alan Hansen – a similar type of player – were the exceptions to the rule.

'Even now we don't have them. If they're put under pressure, they'll lose the ball. Our whole thinking has been based on what's within this island – and that's because we have central defenders who aren't comfortable on the ball. So, in our game, if you go in and close them down, and pressurise the ball, you win it back. But then we come up against these Continental players who have so much skill, and if your first player goes in to close an opponent down to pressurise him and he beats you, they're through you like a knife through butter.

'And that's the problem. They can pressurise our defenders and win the ball back, and the Brazilians, for example, can certainly play a pressurising game. And so can the Dutch. They get behind the ball and all go together and close the ball down. This sort of consideration is important. If you give the ball away playing against Brazil, you don't get it back. Good players can't get it back against them – so ordinary players have got no chance.'

Some would say the newest generation of central defenders and midfielders are at last offering some hope: the names of John Terry, Ledley King and Frank Lampard come to mind. Some would argue so do Sol Campbell and Rio Ferdinand.

In 1996, Paul Power was uniquely well qualified to judge. In 1995, the former Manchester City, Everton and England B player visited half a dozen Continental countries, including Italy, Sweden and Germany, on a fact-finding mission for the PFA report. The report concluded that English soccer urgently needed a wholesale shake-up at club, but more importantly, at schools level and that coaching was central to this. It urged a coaching development programme to ensure the game had a constant stream of technically excellent youngsters coming through in the future. The main obstacle to change was identified as the obsession with the elite stratum of top-paid professionals – to the detriment of youth.

As Paul Power saw it: 'The more forward-looking manager still has a problem in convincing people of the long-term view, especially his board, who think, "Well, ten years is a long time, isn't it?" A lot of clubs are more concerned with how many Mars bars they're going to sell in their shops than they are with a development programme. That's how short-sighted we are. They'd rather go for the cast-offs – from Manchester City, Liverpool, Everton, Manchester United – than invest in their own programme. Their argument is that these clubs are going to get the best players anyway – so who's going to want to come to Bury or Rochdale? So we're only going to be developing third-rate players – that's their thoughts. Now, I would say if you get quality coaches in, and a good structure – like Dario Gradi has at Crewe Alexandra – then it doesn't matter whether you're Crewe or Manchester United; if you look after the players, you'll get the best [at that club].'

There have been many inquiries into the state of the English game, but perhaps none more worrying than *A Kick in the Right Direction*'s claim that English coaching lacked charisma, was out of touch and stagnating. As a result, too many players were deficient in creativity and technical ability, particularly in the passing and dribbling skills necessary to unlock organised defences.

The report involved a two-year comparative survey of English and Continental coaching methods from primary schools up to senior professional club level. The working party included Howard Kendall, Dave Sexton, Steve Heighway, Mick Wadsworth, Eric Harrison, John Cartwright and Micky Burns. Other contributors were Terry Venables, Don Howe, Graham Taylor, Bobby Robson, Andy Roxburgh and Gérard Houllier, then France's national director of coaching.

The English FA's more recent changes to coaching regimes are encouraging, especially in view of the British game's earlier resistance to adopt Continental methods, but perhaps don't go far enough. In 1993, Danish physiologist Jens Bangsbo produced a seminal study on the physiology of football fitness after comparing different training regimes. His conclusion was that there was no difference in the heart rate achieved by players running round a track and that registered by players in three-against-three small soccer games. The message was that the same fitness levels could be achieved just as well by training with the ball as without it.

As Power remarked in 1996: 'Bangsbo suggested to the English FA that they might use his book as a sort of blueprint for coaching and fitness programmes, but the offer was declined. So we didn't include any of that information in our coaching qualifications. We ignored it. But others didn't – the Danes, Swedes, Norwegians, Italians. It has been translated into most languages and has been adopted as the basis for most other countries' coaching and training programmes.'

A small but significant improvement would be to encourage more senior players to undertake coaching educational courses, in order to help improve the standard of soccer tuition generally. But this would require clubs and national associations to be committed to paying them a decent wage. As Power said: 'I think that senior professionals would be really comfortable in this environment, but we've never incorporated into our coach education programme that ability, that understanding of the growth patterns, the psychological development of adolescents and even younger lads, as they have done on the Continent. But it's no use developing coaching qualifications to produce better coaches if the club chairmen don't hire these guys and pay them a decent wage because they're properly qualified. Our substandard coaches have the old mentality where the club thinks, "We'll give him a sponge and get him to manage the team." They think like grocers.

'On the Continent, no coach can work at club level without proper qualifications, and professional club first-team managers in most countries must have a licence. In England, only a basic preliminary qualification is needed to be able to teach in a Centre of Excellence. And coaching 16 to 18 year olds requires no qualifications at all. Anyone can do it. It's all left to chance; it's hit and miss.' No wonder the talent isn't produced, and the PFA report can conclude: 'The British supporter believes players should be committed to the winning cause by showing pace and constant effort rather than complicated or fancy footwork. There needs to be a switch of emphasis from the direct physical approach to one of entertaining, skilful forward play.'

It has taken ten years for the new approaches to make an

impact on the English game through the emergence of a raft of promising younger players. Ten years ago, while championing such changes, the indefatigable Charlie Mitten suggested a simple change of stratgey which coaches at leading clubs could adopt to devastating effect.

# 18

# On Angel Wings

The English game is 30 years behind the rest of the world.
Sepp Blatter, president of FIFA since 1998

THE SATURDAY AFTER CHARLIE MITTEN WAS DISMISSED, Newcastle entertained Brighton at St James' Park and ran out 5–0 winners. 'Charlie's Ghost Returns' screamed the *Daily Mirror*'s back page – and to prove it, an accompanying four-column photograph showed an eerie, unrecognisable figure in a Homburg hat scurrying up the terraces at St James' Park, a picture retoucher's thick black arrow marking the spot. Newcastle had taken eight points from their last five games: won 4–1 v. Luton; lost 0–2 at Liverpool; won 4–1 v. Charlton; won 2–7 at Bury; won 5–0 v. Brighton. The match report made it clear that the real shadow of Charlie Mitten was out on the pitch. 'Newcastle turned on an exhibition which left many people asking what Charlie Mitten had been sacked for. Everything he strived, fought for and represented came off in this match. This team performance was well and truly stamped with the old boss's personality.'

Cheeky Charlie was rumoured to have left St James' Park smiling, but no one knew for sure; for once in his life, Mitten had nothing to say to the press. The team spoke for itself – it was that magic blend of experience and youth and included five of Charlie's youngsters: Heslop, Dalton, Neale, Hale and the electrifying right-winger, Alan Suddick. Mitten's vision of the game was beginning to come good. Two weeks later, he was smiling for all to see – at Filbert Street as his son John helped take Wolves apart with a scintillating display of wing-play for Leicester City. The *Daily Sketch* reported: 'The 20-year-old outside-left is a carbon copy of his father in his Old Trafford prime – the same devastating bursts; the same uncanny positioning; and the same lethal left foot.'

Both John and Charlie, jun. had been members of Newcastle's FA Youth Cup-winning team. And both, along with the host of other youngsters their father brought on at Newcastle, were schooled in the simple secret which he believed to be a prerequisite for soccer success – the ability to dribble and beat a man. All other technique considerations, he believed, were secondary. Never has the need been greater for English football to rediscover this elemental skill. And nowhere could it be deployed to more devastating effect, insisted Charlie Mitten, than on the wings. (If proof of this were needed you need look no further than Sean Wright-Phillips, the home-grown Premiership player who, in my opinion, comes closest to the playing style and skills of Mitten in his pomp.)

In winning soccer's ultimate trophy with his team of 'wingless wonders', Ramsey may have inadvertently condemned English football to a generation in the soccer wilderness, as the game nationally forgot the wonders that can be worked on the wings as nowhere else. Ramsey himself knew precisely what he was doing and why, as Charlie recalled: 'I was sitting next to Alf at a reception dinner after a friendly between United and Benfica, and we got talking about no-winger tactics. Ramsey says to me, "Charlie, find me two English wingers of international quality and I will play them in the national team." He didn't believe there was one player good enough for the role. Alf had to plan tactics for a winning team with no wingers – and deserved all the praise for winning the World Cup.'

But ultimately, raiding wing-play, according to Mitten, was the neglected tactic to beat organised defences, the antidote to spoiling tactics based on physical strength and super-fitness.

Only twice in 46 years has the nation made the last four teams in any major tournament held outside England. Back in 1995, Sepp Blatter, then chief executive officer of FIFA, reckoned England was 30 years behind the rest of the world, and Charlie Mitten agreed. Travelling the globe for UEFA for more than 20 years arranging exhibition friendlies for, among others, Benfica, Manchester United, Chelsea and Nottingham Forest, Charlie was able to see some of the world's leading teams in action at first hand. What struck him was the success of those teams who relied on attacking wingers.

'If you have two well-drilled sides who are making space and marking men, the only way to break out of that deadlock is for one man to create space by beating another – and where is there the most space to do this? On the wing! That's the way I've always felt. I've often asked managers why they take the wingers out of football – and have been told, "Because we need them in defence." So why do they at the same time make their full-backs wingers? It's so contradictory! Herrera was the first to do this, and when I met him in Barcelona once, I said to him that his system was based on weakness. Because he didn't have the players, he devised a system where they'd give nothing away. That wasn't very good for football. Everybody copied him, because they could see he was getting points away from home.'

The Italian *catenaccio* system and its variants finally bit the dust in Lisbon in 1967 when Celtic gloriously destroyed Herrera's Inter Milan to win the European Cup and prove that no defensive soccer strategy was proof against raiding wing-play. The Italians, like everyone else, took the lesson to heart. Everyone, that is, except England – but then, the wingless wonders had won the World Cup. England stopped producing wingers. Charlie recalled that raiding wingers were the secret of Fulham's free-scoring forward line during his days at Craven Cottage.

'At Fulham, Arthur Stevens was a natural outside-right who could cross the ball from the wing straight to a man no bother, every time – a skill that's lost today. They just kick it across now, hoof it to hell. And they can't even kick it properly – because they're not being trained. I'm not decrying all coaches, but the majority are trainers of stamina. They don't realise that skill and stamina go together. Especially when you're trying to run at 100 mph and do something with the ball, because the chap behind you, one of your own teammates, is only doing 50 mph, maybe. Not everyone's built the same, are they? They can't keep up with you. Instead, they should slow it down and make sure everybody is a good ball player – then you can get a nice machine going. Di Stefano would never run at 100 mph – he made people play instead. Within a 20-yard circle around him, he made everybody buzz. And his first touch was brilliant. That's when you kill that ball dead, ready for action, no bobbling around. When players want to pull the ball down, it's often the best of three, isn't it? Two or three touches to get control. How often have you seen a player kill the ball dead first time, or on his thigh on the run? I used to do that and they'd say, "Don't do that too often, they'll be kicking you there!" How can they be kicking me when it's given me the chance to put ten yards between myself and my marker? Players can't do it today because they've never been shown – 75 per cent of what they do in training is running, running, running. Some days at certain clubs, players never touch the ball for individual skill training. It's all "get after the ball, chase it till it stops rolling". Most managers and coaches say they want fitness. But if you've got a player who

248

hasn't got ball skills first, what the bloody hell's the use of teaching him anything else? And yet such tactics can put the team top of their division. It makes you wonder what the hell's the rest of the division doing; what's the quality of the football being played, if this way can be such a success?

'Taking the ball, controlling it and turning all in one movement is the most basic skill any footballer should have – the so-called Hungarian turn. But how many players in the Premiership have you seen do it? Half a dozen maybe. And if *they* can do it, why can't the others? Is it considered too fancy, or of no value?

'It's this sort of skill on the ball, and the ability and willingness to run at defences, which allows you to take apart any system of defence. And it's on the wings that it can be most effectively deployed – because out wide it not only creates space but it also stretches a defence. So a good coach should be looking for this talent and natural ability and be ringing it out. You *can* have useful players that don't cost millions.

'The whole world is looking for the next Eusébio, Pelé, Best. But when they say they're looking for these stars, they don't realise they're here, underneath our own feet. So we come to another problem in football: the quality of person looking for these youngsters. A first-class scout is a football club's best friend – if he knows what he's doing. But 90 per cent of scouts today don't know what they're looking for.'

It was Charlie's uncompromising view that if players didn't have the basic ball-playing skills – trapping, shooting and being able to kick a ball properly – they shouldn't be playing football no matter how fit they were. Perhaps that explained England's poor record at international level.

'Look at Ajax. They've got a brilliant team there that's virtually representing their country – a country as small as Holland. And yet these countries can seem to find the players. They approach things differently. In Holland, they've got superb facilities for their young 17 year olds – fields, sport centres and organised coaching everywhere. I've been there, I've seen it.

'In this country, we've now got sports centres for the elite – at Lilleshall. We may have the buildings and facilities, but what about the quality of the teaching? There is some work on ball skills and techniques, the skills of the game, but not enough. It's all about the ball. If all 11 players in a team can manipulate that ball, you'll fill the stands. Don't they understand? Why shouldn't defenders be just as skilled? Dribbling, beating a man, crossing the ball accurately? Sticking it in the net is not just for forwards. We've got to end this rigid division between ball-playing forwards and tough, hard-man defenders. Of course, everybody isn't going to be a Best or a Pelé or a Giggs. But there's no reason I can see why every man in a team shouldn't be, ought to be, a good player on the ball. Otherwise he's no right to be on the pitch. Unless this attitude changes, we in this country are never going to match the rest of the world. I learned that in Bogotá. I was up against players who were as good as me and as pacey, and I thought to myself, "Charles, you've got to beat him." I'd got to learn a trick or two to beat my marker; a trick for the occasion; dribbling skills.'

Charlie believed that what was destroying football creativity was a fear among the players of losing the ball, of getting beaten by an opposing player. Much better to get rid of the ball and take no prisoners. And yet it's no secret – dribbling with the ball is a way to win matches, it's very simple. But this 'secret' went missing, the element of creativity, the ability to beat a man.

'If your players can't dribble, your team will be less good, less creative, less likely to win. The point is that beating one, or two, or three men opens up the chances for someone to score goals. And that's the point of the game. But you have to be technically able to do it instinctively. The ability to beat a man is a skill that has to be polished in training, and you've got to have a coach who recognises it. In training, it's polishing that blend of pace, control and dribble. You keep doing it, doing it, going past the man, so that you know, are sure, you can do it every time.

'It's the same with shooting and crossing the ball. When I was a youngster of 17 at United, I was told to pinpoint the ball when I centred it. So I asked how I was supposed to do that. The coach, Harry Ablett, took the corner flagpoles and stuck them in the six-yard box and said, "Hit the tops of the flags every time you cross – not the middle of the bloody stick, that's the man's chest. Put it on top, that's his head, he'll do the rest." That's polishing the gifts you've got.

'Each player has a different level of individual skill; very few are gifted with total mastery of all. But everyone can work to perfect those he has. I would rank the most important skills as (1) first-touch perfect ball control; (2) dribbling ability to beat a man; (3) tactical vision; (4) total coordination of brain and foot in passing and shooting. Technique comes easier with constant practice, especially when you polish those skills used to best effect in your position during a match. But the basic skills of dribbling, passing and shooting should be practised on a daily, routine basis with your favourite foot, and sprint-starting at least three times a week. In developing a team with skilful ball-players, the service to forwards can become almost perfect.'

Having analysed what he saw as the weaknesses in the English game and the deficiencies in coaching regimes which he believed were to blame, Charlie Mitten, ever the football thinker, came up with a novel solution: specialist coaches for every position on the field. The 'Harley Street specialists of soccer', he thought, could be the saving of the English game.

'The reasons why we have so few top-class wingmen today are that most coaches are ignorant of the skills and subtleties required, and what you don't know, you can't teach. It stands to reason that even where a coach has been a player, unless he's been a winger or centre-back or goalkeeper or striker himself, he will not have that instinctive knowledge to impart about a particular position he has never played in. No matter how good a player he was, in almost all cases his knowledge will be too general. The answer is specialised coaches. So, if a manager feels a player needs to develop a certain skill or skills, he could send the lad to a specialist – just like in the medical profession where your GP might refer you to a consultant, an expert in a certain field, who can "fix" your problem.'

Both of his sons, Charlie felt, had definite promise. When he left the Newcastle manager's chair to become a licensed UEFA agent, both went to other clubs, but things didn't quite work out for either. John had a couple of seasons at Leicester and a few months at Manchester United before moving via Coventry and Plymouth Argyle to Exeter City, where he finished his playing days. Charlie, jun., also finished up in the West Country – at Argyle – after spells at Bury, Halifax and, initially, Leeds, where he impressed Don Revie. Their father is brutally honest about both of his sons.

'John had everything and a lovely left peg, except he was short of pace. But as the game changed, he could have switched to midfield and been a great success. He was a lot like the former Arsenal star, Liam Brady. Charlie had it all – the zip, the shot, everything. But Don Revie used to ring me up and say, "The lad's brilliant up to half-time, Charles, but he disappears after that." So we got a specialist in – and it was his asthma, he couldn't find the wind; he died after half-time. It broke his heart; he was only 19. It was a shame – he would have been a really good player. Now it's all down to his son Paul – my grandson – to carry on the family tradition.'

Paul Mitten was signed by Manchester United as a schoolboy while starring for a Cheadle junior side in the Stockport area league, but was not retained after a cruciate ligament injury. On his recovery, he had games for several north-west clubs including Crewe, Bury and Stockport, before being signed for Coventry by Ron Atkinson. At the age of 19, he'd played half a dozen games in the reserves in season 1995–96 before another injury put him out of action.

Charlie always liked to keep up with the big matches on TV and with the fortunes of the club he helped to make great, Manchester United. But even Cheeky Charlie could never have foreseen how the illustrious Mitten name would be caught up in a new soccer drama at the Theatre of Dreams.

# Epilogue

FOR STEPHEN HAWKING TIME HAS JUST GOT BRIEFER, proving what those old proverbs have long maintained: time and tide wait for no man, and the past often comes full circle. If Charlie Mitten's sons failed honourably to quite cut it in the style of their dad, the Mitten soccer bloodline nevertheless looks set to go on.

And even more intriguingly, Manchester United is once again at the heart of the matter.

The £790 million takeover at Old Trafford by 'Glazers US, Inc.' ruffled quite a few feathers – not least in the Mitten extended-family coop. Disaffected supporters who have heroically set up their own team – FC United of Manchester – as the first step towards creating another Theatre of Dreams, have been making headlines not just for their brass-necked cheek. They've succeeded in signing up not one Mitten, but two – great-grandson Charlie and great-nephew Jonathan – to play for them in the North-West Counties League. That's nine rungs down from the Premiership and several tens of thousand fewer spectators for games at their shared home ground: Bury's Gigg Lane.

Jonathan – or 'Jozza' as he's popularly known – has all the feisty élan of his illustrious forebear and like him played for Altrincham before switching loyalties. As I suggested 18 chapters ago, you couldn't make this stuff up. I'll resist the temptation to suggest what Cheeky Charlie would have made of it – but I'm sure you can guess.

Charlie was also impressed, it must be said, with the two young Man City starlets who did his blindfold-penalty theory proud all those years ago. They obviously didn't make it to the big time with City, but I recall seeing them play in the first team, and I thought they were good prospects. Certainly their current teams must think so. However, I'd wager a ten bob note to one of Charlie's greyhounds that they've never let on to their new teammates about the feats they performed that day. They wouldn't believe you? Tell 'em a TV crew filmed the whole thing. It was just that it was never broadcast in this country. Well, lads, you didn't think it was going to stay a secret – or did you? No need to be bashful – I'm still gobsmacked by what I saw you pull off. And I never did thank you personally. Let me make amends now: Jeff Whitley of Cardiff City and Lee Crooks of Bradford City, many thanks. If you can do it, why the hell can't all those millionaire galacticos?

Finally, before I wind this up, I can't resist revealing the best-kept secret at Arsenal for the past 25 years – why clever clogs George Graham never made it as a youngster in Charlie's famous youth side at Newcastle? Ask him and he'll tell you: 'It's because I was too busy walking Charlie Mitten's greyhounds.' (Thanks to Charlie's journalist nephew Andy Mitten for that one. Cheers Andy!)